Pachappa Camp

KOREAN COMMUNITIES ACROSS THE WORLD

Series Editor
Joong-Hwan Oh, Hunter College, CUNY

Korean Communities across the World publishes works that address aspects of (a) the Korean American community, (b) Korean society, (c) the Korean communities in other foreign lands, or (d) transnational Korean communities. In the field of (a) the Korean American community, this series welcomes contributions involving concepts such as Americanization, pluralism, social mobility, migration/immigration, social networks, social institutions, social capital, racism/discrimination, settlement, identity, or politics, as well as a specific topic related to family/marriage, gender roles, generations, work, education, culture, citizenship, health, ethnic community, housing, ethnic identity, racial relations, social justice, social policy, and political views, among others. In the field of (b) Korean society, this series embraces scholarship on current issues such as gender roles, age/ aging, low fertility, immigration, urbanization, gentrification, economic inequality, high youth unemployment, sexuality, democracy, political power, social injustice, the nation's educational problems, social welfare, capitalism, consumerism, labor, health, housing, crime, environmental degradation, and the social life in the digital age and its impacts, among others. Contributors in the field of (c) Korean communities in other foreign lands are encouraged to submit works that expand our understanding about the formation, vicissitudes, and major issues of an ethnic Korean community outside of South Korea and the Unites States, such as cultural or linguistic retention, ethnic identity, assimilation, settlement patterns, citizenship, economic activities, family relations, social mobility, and racism/discrimination. Lastly, contributions relating to (d) transnational Korean communities may touch upon transnational connectivity in family, economy/finance, politics, culture, technology, social institutions, and people.

Pachappa Camp

The First Koreatown in the United States

Edward T. Chang

LEXINGTON BOOKS
Lanham • Boulder • New York • London

Published by Lexington Books
An imprint of The Rowman & Littlefield Publishing Group, Inc.
4501 Forbes Boulevard, Suite 200, Lanham, Maryland 20706
www.rowman.com

6 Tinworth Street, London SE11 5AL, United Kingdom

British Library Cataloguing in Publication Information Available

Library of Congress Cataloging-in-Publication Data

Library of Congress Control Number: 2021932002

Contents

Acknowledgments

This book is my twelfth publication and the most gratifying research project I have been involved with over the last thirty years. Several years ago, Korean American students at UC Riverside found a map published by the Sanborn Insurance Company of New York in 1908. The map of downtown Riverside near Pachappa Ave, included a caption "Korean settlement." I had never heard of the existence of the Korean community in Riverside during the early twentieth century. It was widely known that Korean immigrants settled in Honolulu, Hawaii; San Francisco; or Los Angeles during the early twentieth century, but not in Riverside, California.

My journey began in 2016 and it was like trying to find a needle in a haystack. At the time, very little literature, writing, or research material on the Riverside Korean community was available. Sunju Lee wrote an article on Pachappa Camp, the Korean settlement in Riverside, but very few pieces of evidence were provided to support his claim. As I searched for any materials or information on the early Korean community in Riverside, I was delighted to find new information here and there. I felt inspiration and joy as I began to piece together the existence of the early Korean community in Riverside. In particular, the Korean language newspapers *Sinhan Minbo* and *Gongnip Sinbo* turned out to be jackpot sources as they provided rich information on the Korean community in Riverside during the early twentieth century.

Jia Yoon and Hyerin Joo, Korean literature Ph.D. students at Korea University, found and translated *Sinhan Minbo* and *Gongnip Sinbo* newspaper articles into modern Korean language. Without their translation of old Korean language to modern Korean language, I would not have been able to carry out and complete this research project without their help. They were god-sent angels who came to the Young Oak Kim (YOK) Center for Korean American Studies at UC Riverside as graduate student interns in 2018. I am greatly indebted to Jia Yoon and Hyerin Joo for their help on this research project.

Special appreciation is extended to supporters of the YOK Center: Dr. Mike Hong and late Lorrie Hong, Steve Ro, Yeung J. Kim, Jay Kim, Han Yeul Cha, Jang Young Jung Johnney Park, John Son, Peter Yoon, Jong Woon Lee, and Kae Hong Ko. They not only supported the YOK Center financially but also provided strong support and encouragement for this research project.

Acknowledgement is also warmly given to Milagros Peña and Sang Hee Lee, a former dean and assistant dean of the College of Humanities, Arts, and Social Sciences, UC Riverside, respectively, for their generous support of the Young Oak Kim Center. My research assistant, Hannah Brown, found many invaluable materials on the early Korean immigrant communities in Riverside and laid the foundation for this research project.

In particular, I would like to express my special appreciation and gratitude to Carol Park, who spent hours correcting early drafts and providing editorial suggestions to improve this manuscript.

Last but certainly not least, I would like to dedicate this book to our family members: Janet, Angie Chang, Kevin Shih, and my father, Ho Chang.

November 2020
Riverside, California
Edward Taehan Chang

Introduction

On March 23, 2017, an official ceremony was held to install a sign marking the site of Pachappa Camp a "Cultural Point of Interest" by City of Riverside.[1] In addition, Dosan Ahn Chang Ho's statue stands tall in downtown Riverside, California, on University Avenue and Main Street. Why, how, and what is the meaning of the Pachappa Camp designation and Dosan Ahn Chang Ho's statue in Riverside, California? Dosan (Island Mountain) is Ahn Chang Ho's penname. Koreans at home and abroad both respect and admire Ahn Chang Ho as one of Korea's most patriotic and dedicated reformers. According to Hyung-Chan Kim, "Ahn Chang Ho was a towering historic figure who dwarfs in significance most Korean nationalists involved in the development of modern Korean nationalism during the period of Japanese colonial domination over Korea that spanned the five decades between 1895 and 1945."[2] Dosan's life story is powerful and contrary to what history has written about him being a pacifist or cultural nationalist; he was actually "a revolutionary-democrat who championed constitutional democracy as demonstrated by his leadership in the Korean independence movement throughout the world."[3] Dosan Ahn Chang Ho is respected for devoting and ultimately giving up his life for Korea's freedom.[4] Ahn famously stated even while being tortured in prison: "Yes, I regard the very act of eating an act on behalf of independence and the very act of sleeping an act on behalf of independence. Until this body is destroyed, I will never be any different."[5] Ahn Chang Ho organized, educated, and mobilized Korean immigrants in the United States. He told Korean immigrants to become good citizens with a sense of civic responsibility to America and Korea. Working as a farmhand in Riverside, California, Dosan told his fellow countrymen to work hard and diligently: "Please pay attention to every single orange you pick. That is the way to help yourself and our country."[6] Ahn helped found the Korean employment agency that attracted Korean immigrants to the city and oversaw the establishment of civic associations. Under Dosan's leadership, the Korean settlement in Riverside grew to become the first Koreatown on the mainland United States, where Koreans lived, worked, organized community events, and developed independence organizations together. The Riverside-based Korean community, called Pachappa Camp, was known as Dosan's Republic and was founded sometime in late 1904 or early 1905.

I was able to trace how and why Pachappa Camp was established and by whom, utilizing several newly discovered primary sources: (1) *San Francisco Chronicle* interview of Dosan Ahn Chang Ho on December 7, 1902, (2) *Gongnip Sinbo* and *Sinhan Minbo* articles provided valuable information on Pachappa Camp and its activities, (3) writings and stories by several scholars and writers on Pachappa Camp, including Hyung-chan Kim's *Tosan Ahn Ch'ang-Ho: A Profile of a Prophetic Patriot*, Mary Paik Lee's *Quiet Odyssey*, John Cha's *Willow Tree Shade: The Susan Ahn Cuddy Story*, Eursark Cha's *Golden Mountain*, and Bong-youn Choy's *Koreans in America*, (4) early records of the Calvary Presbyterian Church of Riverside shed new light on the Pachappa Korean mission and its activities, (5) *Riverside Daily Press* and local newspaper articles helped characterize and understand the lives of the residents of Pachappa Camp and their relations with other communities, (6) I was able to identify the names of Pachappa Camp residents using 1910 and 1920 U.S. census records, and (7) U.S. Immigration file on Dosan Ahn Chang Ho (1924–1926) provided invaluable information on how and why Ahn was deported by the U.S. Immigration Service Office in March 1926. Many of these primary source materials are newly discovered and shed new light on not only the formation of Pachappa Camp, but also on the buried past of early Korean American history.

On August 11, 2001, several hundred Korean Americans gathered to celebrate the erection of the Dosan Ahn Chang Ho Memorial Statue in Riverside, California. Dosan Ahn Chang Ho spent roughly thirteen years in the United States and lived in Riverside more than five years (1904–1907 and 1911–1913). Dosan travelled extensively throughout the United States, and his family resided in Riverside until they moved to Los Angeles sometime in October 1913. While residing in the city, Dosan established the *Gongnip Hyop Hoe* (Cooperative Association) and initiated the idea of establishing the New People's Association (*Siminhoe)* in Korea.[7] Dosan also developed the basis for the *HeungSaDan*, the Young Korean Academy, in Riverside, an association Dosan founded in San Francisco in 1913 to develop leaders for an independent Korea. Furthermore, the Korean National Association of North America held its National Convention in Riverside in 1911 right after Dosan came back to America from one of his multiple trips to Korea. Riverside further proves a central location in the Korean independence movement because of the community organizations Ahn established in the city. As I will prove later, I strongly believe that Dosan Ahn Chang Ho and the *Gongnip Hyophoe* devised plans to relocate newly arriving Korean immigrants from Hawaii and China and settle them in Riverside.

It is no accident that Riverside's Pachappa Camp was a family-based community, unlike other Korean settlements. And yet, Riverside, California, is nearly absent from Dosan Ahn Chang Ho's history and biography. The famous biography of Dosan by Lee Kwang Soo does not even mention Riverside.[8] In addition, the city is mostly absent from the online exhibit of Dosan's life at the Dosan Memorial Foundation located in Gangnam-gu, Seoul, Korea. The Young Korean Academy (*HeungSaDan*), also fails to include Dosan's life and legacy in Riverside, California, on its website. Because the Koreatown did not survive, the migrant workers' propensity to move, as well as the Ahn family's relocation to Los Angeles in 1913, Riverside's central place in Korean American history has been overlooked.

Dosan's life in America took place in three different periods: (1) 1902–1907, (2) 1911–1919, and (3) 1924–1926. Dosan Ahn Chang Ho and his wife, Hyeryon (Helen) arrived in San Francisco on October 14, 1902, via Honolulu, Vancouver, and Seattle. He stayed in San Francisco for less than a year and a half and decided to relocate to Riverside, California, in 1904. Employment opportunities and climate were among the many reasons why he decided to relocate to Riverside. Dosan Ahn Chang Ho established the Korean Labor Bureau in late 1904 or early 1905 and provided employment services to newly arriving Korean immigrants. Soon, Riverside became the destination of Korean immigrants, and Pachappa Camp was established, which grew rapidly. Pachappa Camp became the first and the largest Koreatown, USA, during the early twentieth century. One of the main purposes of this book is to trace how and why Pachappa Camp was established and uncover how it became the center of the early Korean immigrant community in America.

Dosan returned to Korea in 1907 in order to engage in secret independence activities by organizing the New People's Society. After Korea was colonized in 1910, Dosan decided to come back to America in 1911 and stayed until 1919. It is important to note that the Third Korean National Association of North America convention was held in Riverside right after Dosan returned to America. Scholars and researchers paid very little attention to the historical importance of the KNA convention held at Riverside in November 1911. Not only did Dosan's family reside in Riverside, but Pachappa Camp was the center of independence activities during the early twentieth century in America. During his second stay in America, Dosan actively travelled and organized Korean Americans throughout the Americas. Dosan's last journey to America was between 1924 and 1926. Until now, scholars and researchers paid very little attention to how and why Dosan Ahn Chang Ho was deported by the U.S. Immigration Service Office in 1926. In this volume, I uncover how and why Dosan was interrogated by the Immigration Office and eventually deported. The focus of this book is the first and last period of Dosan Ahn Chang Ho's time in America.

Also, I intend to pinpoint Riverside, California, as one of the most important historical sites of Dosan Ahn Chang Ho's life in America.[9] More importantly, I argue that Pachappa Camp or Dosan's Republic, the two colloquial names for the site located in downtown Riverside, should be known as the first Koreatown in the United States. In addition, Pachappa Camp became the largest Koreatown in America during the early 1900s. Koreans lived scattered throughout cities, including San Francisco and Honolulu, and had not established their own distinct organized neighborhoods, like they did in Riverside.[10] Also, in Hawaii, Korean immigrants lived and worked on plantation property and had no distinct organized community of their own. The Korean Methodist Mission was established in November 1903, however, its members listed mostly Ewha Plantation as their home addresses. Thus, Koreans in Hawaii had no formal organized-Korean settlement of their own at the time. Also, it is important to note that Koreans used San Francisco as a port of entry and as a temporary site where they could gather information about other cities and locations in the United States. San Francisco housed Korean organizations and churches in various locations, but the community had no formalized Koreatown or settlement. In fact, Koreans who landed in San Francisco faced strong anti-Asian sentiment and left the bustling port city because of a lack of job opportunities. In fact, an article published in the *Sinhan Minbo* (October 5, 1910) confirmed that Pachappa Camp is the first Korean settlement in the United States.

> Riverside is the first Korean village (*Dong-nae*) in the United States. In addition, the first Korean National Association local chapter was established in Riverside. It was uncertain if the Riverside Korean community can maintain itself as many Korean laborers moved frequently to other places. However, Mr. In Soo Kim and his family settled in Riverside and provided leadership in maintaining the Korean settlement. And his son, YongRyun, negotiated rent for Korean workers. Mr. In Soo Kim paid for the shortage of the Community Center maintenance fund.

According to the *Sihan Minbo* article, Riverside's Pachappa Camp was not only the first Korean settlement in the United States, but also the location of the first local chapter of the Korean National Association. It was not an accident that the first Koreatown was established in Riverside, California.

Ahn Chang Ho and the *Gongnip Hyophoe* devised plans to relocate Korean immigrants who landed in San Francisco to Riverside. Korean residents in Riverside urged Dosan Ahn Chang Ho to move back to San Francisco to help newly arriving Korean immigrants to settle in America in 1905. In addition, residents of Pachappa Camp told Dosan that they will provide financial support and that he should concentrate on establishing the headquarters of the *Gongnip Hyophoe* in San Francisco. According to Bong-youn Choy, "The plan was as follows. Physically strong and experienced Koreans are to be sent to the Riverside orchards as a sample labor force. They are told to construct their own living quarters as soon as they arrived, without asking for any money from Americans. Then they are to organize a working team of ten men."[11] Choy also explained that Korean workers were provided lunch boxes, and train tickets, and the leaders of *Gongnip Hyophoe* told the conductor the name of the station where they were to get off.[12] Ahn Chang Ho dreamt of establishing a Korean community governed by democratic principles with rules and regulations in Riverside, California. Unlike other temporary Korean camps mostly of young single males, Pachappa Camp was a family-based community of men, women, and children. With plans to relocate Korean immigrants to Pachappa, the number of *Gongnip Hyophoe* members at Pachappa increased from seventy in 1905 to 150 in 1907.[13,14] If you include women and children, Pachappa Camp housed more than two hundred Korean immigrants as of 1907.

In Riverside, CA, Pachappa Camp grew around the Korean Labor Bureau (1904 or 1905), which aided Koreans in finding jobs primarily in agriculture in the region. With work readily available, Koreans at Pachappa Camp launched a number of community activities, including a Korean Presbyterian mission with help from the Calvary Presbyterian Church, social organizations such as the *Gongnip Hyophoe*, discussion groups, and later on Korean language schools. Because of the combination of these factors—its sizeable population, centralized living quarters, and the presence of community organizations and businesses—Pachappa Camp meets the criteria for an ethnic enclave as laid out by sociologist Mark Abrahamson.[15] Ahn Chang Ho wanted to build a model Korean immigrant community in Riverside where Koreans had a place to live, work, worship, learn, discuss, and carry out independence activities. As I will explain later more in detail, Ahn Chang Ho gave specific instructions to Korean immigrant laborers to work "honestly" picking oranges, so other Korean workers could find employment.

According to Sunju Lee, who first wrote about Pachappa Camp in Korean language in 2003, "Riverside was the most important base of Dosan Ahn Chang Ho's life in America and yet researchers and scholars failed to understand the historical importance of Pachappa Camp."[16] Sun Joo Lee believed that Dosan and his family relocated to Los Angeles during early 1914; however, they moved to Los Angeles in December 1913.[17] Pachappa Camp in Riverside was the center of the early Korean independence movement and served as a base camp for Korean immigrant laborers. And yet, its historical importance has not been much known, studied, and understood. What are the reasons researchers and scholars paid very little attention to the historical importance of Riverside's Pachappa Camp in early Korean American history? Instead, Dosan Ahn Chang Ho's biography and activities focus on San Francisco and Los Angeles. One of the reasons could be that the headquarters of the *Gongnip Hyophoe* and the Korean National Association were located in San Francisco and later moved to Los Angeles. Dosan Ahn Chang Ho also registered as a member of either the San Francisco or Los Angeles chapter member of the KNA, not Riverside. I intend to locate Riverside's Pachappa Camp as not only the first and largest Koreatown but also the mecca of early Korean independence movement.

Koreans at Pachappa Camp formed a sense of community and cohesion unprecedented in other Korean American populations. Koreans at Pachappa were not insular, and they forged inter-ethnic relations with the Chinese and Anglo populations of Riverside. In the following text, I intend to explore these questions: (1) Why and how did Dosan establish Pachappa Camp in Riverside, California? (2) What was the historical importance and the significance of Pachappa Camp in the Korean American independence movement? (3) Why is it important to understand the role of Pachappa Camp in Korean American history? (4) What is the significance of erecting Dosan's Statue in Riverside, California, and how can I utilize it for education of second-generation Korean Americans and young people? Furthermore, I hope to draw attention to areas in need of further research in Dosan's life, particularly his early years when he first came to the United States.

Below is a brief timeline of Dosan's major activities in the United States.

October 14, 1902	Ahn Chang Ho and his wife arrived in San Francisco from Hawaii via Vancouver and Seattle
March 23, 1094	Ahn Chang Ho Arrived in Riverside
1905	*Gongnip Hyophoe* and Korean Labor Bureau are established
1905	(Korean Mission) –
1906	*Sinminhoe* Initiated
November 22, 1922	Korean National Association of North America Convention
November 1918	KNA of Riverside relocated to 1158 Vine Street

In addition, I intend to fill the void of research about the last journey of Dosan Ahn Chang Ho to America (1924–1926). Based on a United States

Immigration Service file on Dosan Ahn Chang Ho, I shed new light on why and how Dosan Ahn Chang Ho was deported by the U.S. Immigration Service Office on March 2, 1926. Based on U.S. Immigration Service documents and *Sinhan Minbo* articles, I firmly conclude that Dosan Ahn Chang Ho was deported by the U.S. Immigration Service Office in 1926, and he was never allowed to be reunited with his family in America. Ralph Ahn, the youngest son of Doan Ahn Chang Ho, has never seen his father, as Dosan left San Francisco on March 2, 1926, while his wife Helen was pregnant. Ahn was arrested by the Japanese police in 1932 in Shanghai and died in 1938, due to harsh imprisonment and torture.

UNDERSTANDING THE ROLE OF PACHAPPA CAMP IN KOREAN AMERICAN HISTORY

Korean American history reaches as far back as 1882 with the signing of the Korean-American Treaty. However, it wasn't until 1883—after the signing of the Treaty of Amity, Commerce and Navigation/Shufeldt Treaty, between Korea and the United States—that an official envoy from Korea visited America. The treaty allowed Koreans to pursue opportunities in the United States and for Americans to enter Korea. The Korean envoy was led by Min Young-ik. He stayed in the United States instead of returning to Korea. Min became the first Korean student to study in America. He studied at the Governor Drummer Academy in Massachusetts.[18] Two years after the first envoy from Korea visited America, another group of Koreans decided to visit the United States. In 1885, Soh Jae Pil, Park Yoeng-hyo, and Suh Gwang-beom boarded a ship and sailed to San Francisco. While Soh Jae Pil stayed in the United States, he was not officially counted by the U.S. government as a Korean immigrant. The first recorded Korean immigrant to the United States is believed to be Peter Ryu; he arrived in Honolulu in 1901.[19] Interestingly, the *Times-Picayune* (New Orleans, Louisiana), reported the arrival of a Korean student with the headline "A Korean Student for America." Surh Beung Kiu came to Roanoke College, Virginia, to study. According to this newspaper report, there was only one other Korean student in America at this time, and he was at the University of Pennsylvania.[20] In the late 1800s, a small number of Korean merchants ventured to the United States to sell ginseng to the Chinese railroad workers in places like San Francisco.

Official Korean immigration to the United States began with the arrival of 121 Korean immigrants from Incheon, Korea, to Honolulu on January 13, 1903. The *San Francisco Call* reported the story on page 1 with the headline, "New Hands Are Expected to Prove Much More Valuable Than the Cubans" on January 14, 1903.

The steamer Gaelic arrived here today from the Orient. In her steerage are 102 Koreans, including twenty-one women. The Koreans will be put to work on the sugar plantations with a view to testing their efficiency as laborers. It is thought that they will accomplish more work than the average plantation laborer, and are expected to prove much more valuable than the Cuban laborers brought here last year. If the laborers arriving today on the Gaelic prove to be profitable [to] employers, there will no doubt be a large influx of Koreans at this port.[21]

Indeed, between 1903 and 1905, approximately 7,226 Korean immigrants came to Hawaii as sugar plantation laborers. Of that number, one thousand Korean immigrants returned back to Korea, unable to cope with the harsh working conditions and low wages. Between 1904 and 1907, approximately one thousand Korean immigrants moved to the mainland United States in search of better working conditions and higher wages. In addition, Korean immigrants from Hawaii decided to relocate to the mainland before implementation of the Gentleman's Agreement that prohibited migration of Japanese people from Hawaii to the U.S. mainland. Korean immigrants were afraid that the United States government would also prohibit migration of Korean immigrants from Hawaii to the mainland. Therefore, the Korean immigrant population in Hawaii declined between 1907 and 1912.[22]

Dosan Ahn Chang Ho returned to Korea between 1907 and 1911 to engage in secret New People's Society activities to gain independence of Korea. After Korea was colonized by Japan in 1910, he returned to Riverside via New York in September 1911. Ahn Chang Ho emphasized the importance of maintaining Korean identity and rejected being labeled as "Japanese subjects." According to Ellen Thun, Dosan Ahn Chang Ho advocated war against Japan, not to arm with guns and rifles but to build educational capital and business enterprise. Thun recounted Dosan's viewpoints in her *Korea Times* newspaper column *Heart Warmers*.

> "How do I go about regaining our country's independence?" Dosan asked himself. In 1907, he related, he had gone to Korea when leaders there realized the seriousness of Japan's intention, which was to take over the country and make it a colony for a stepping stone to conquer all of Asia. But that was a future problem to face. Important right now, he said, is to keep Korean consciousness alive. Korea for the Koreans! Not a Japanized Korea, because that meant slavery. Rather a democracy peopled by self-reliant citizens who felt a personal responsibility for the country."[23]

Dosan returned to Riverside in 1911 to organize, mobilize, and urge fellow Korean immigrants in the United States to engage in the independence movement. The experiences of the Koreans who lived at Pachappa Camp—Dosan's Republic—reflect not only exceptional moments in Korean American history but also the ubiquitous experiences that typified immigrant lives in the United States. Immigrants from Asia experienced discrimination in both the types of jobs they could acquire and in the wages they received. From fruit-picking and packing, working in cement foundries, to cooking, serving, and cleaning in hotels and homes, Koreans had little opportunity to amass wealth from their labors. Working in Riverside often served as a steppingstone for families to move on to independent sharecropping, as seen with the Paiks and Chung Sup Park's family, who moved to Northern California to farm after residing a few years in Riverside. The labor bureau allowed migrant workers to find jobs, and the boarding house provided them a safe place to stay. Community activities that took place at Pachappa Camp also reflect larger trends in Korean American history, such as the importance of church. Church for many Koreans represented their only break from work and an opportunity to socialize in addition to its spiritual uplift. The establishment of a Korean Mission in Riverside attests to the importance of the church in this community's life. The Korean community of Riverside also proved especially sensitive to economic push and pull factors: a freeze in 1913 prompted a large decline in population, as orange pickers found themselves out of work before a decimated crop and sought other opportunities in cities such as Los Angeles that could support a greater number of service workers than could Riverside.

The residents' relations with community members also reveal larger trends in Korean American history. Individuals experienced both hardships and charity, from being called "Chinaman," to receiving doll donations, being invited to church, or given help learning English. Their experiences reveal both the extreme poverty in which they lived, and the ranging receptions they received from Americans and other immigrants. They benefited from the help of a generous few who welcomed them to the United States and struggled with the animosity of others. Before establishing Dosan's Republic, many Korean immigrants experienced isolation due to communication barriers, and cultural misunderstandings. Having a Koreatown in Riverside, a place to gather and organize, helped stabilize a largely migrant community. As the first and the largest Koreatown, Pachappa Camp could also put the ideals of the *Gongnip Hyophoe* to task, forging a sense of order, unity, and pride among the Korean community. The strong ties Koreans established through this association underline the importance of Pachappa's residents in the fight for independence. As the home of Dosan Ahn Chang Ho, it became one of the central locations in the independence movement, as revealed by its hosting of the 1911 Korean National Association of North America Delegates Convention, the year after Japan colonized Korea.

The camp was known throughout California as a place to live, work, learn, and fight for independence. All of these factors give enduring value to Dosan's

Republic, which reach beyond each individual resident's experiences to members of other communities both past and present. Whether an individual studies agriculture, labor movements, nationalism, sociology, history, linguistics, or even statistics, he or she can gain value from studying this location. In this volume, I hope to fill the void in Dosan Ahn Chang Ho's legacy in America, modern Korean independence history, and Korean American history.

NOTES

1. Pachapa is a known site with a deep historical narrative, but it was the last documented and excavated qawiyah site in this region. John Goodman has given many lectures on his archeological work at Pachapa, also historically designated "Spring Rancherla" in his written report. It is situated in the downtown Riverside area, and studies indicate that it is the closest qawiyah village site to campus, occupied till the turn of the century. Its collection is curated at Riverside Metropolitan Museum, where an exhibit that John helped with was curated until the closure of the museum. Additionally, pictures exist of the site from the 1800s and are currently held by the museum.

2. Hyung-chan Kim, *Tosan Ahn Ch'ang-Ho: A Profile of a Prophetic Patriot*. Seoul, Korea: Tosan Memorial Foundation, 1996: Preface.

3. Jacqueline Pak, "An Ch'angho and the Nationalist Origins of Korean Democracy," (Ph.D. diss., School of Oriental and African Studies, University of London, 1999).

4. Ahn Chang Ho died in 1938 from complications due to his imprisonment by Japanese colonial authorities. He was first arrested in 1932 and served three years in prison, and was arrested a second time in 1937. He was charged both times for violating Japan's Peace Preservation Law, which allowed Japan to hold individuals accountable for any anti-Japanese activities even on foreign territories.

5. Quoted in Hyung-chan Kim, *Tosan Ahn Ch'ang-Ho: A Profile of a Prophetic Patriot* (Los Angeles: Academia Koreana, 1996), 267.

6. Yo-han Chu, Ahn Tosan Cheonseo (The Complete Works of Ahn Ch'ang-ho), (Seoul: Samchungtang, 1963), 48.

7. The Cooperative Association is also known as the Mutual Assistance Association.

8. Kwang Soo Lee, *Dosan Ahn Chang Ho* (Seoul: HeungSaDan, 1947).

9. See Sun Joo Lee's article Dosan's Activities in Riverside: 1904–1914. In *The Independence Movement and Its Outgrowth by Korean Americans*. Los Angeles: Centennial Committee of Korean Immigration to the U.S. 2003: 111–192.

10. Marn Cha and Andrew Cha also argue Reedley and Dinuba California Ire the first Koreatowns on the United States mainland, but both those Korean communities came into being in the 1910s, several years after Pachappa Camp.

11. Bong-youn Choy, *Koreans in America*. Chicago: Nelson Hall, 1979: 106.

12. *Ibid*, 106–107.

13. *Gongnip Sinbo*, December 21, 1905: 4.

14. Gongnip Sinbo, June 7, 1907.

15. Abrahamson argues that ethnic enclaves have high ethnic homogeneity as well as shared cultural capital and economic interests. See *Urban Enclaves: Identity and Place in America* (St. Martin's Press, 1996).

16. Sun Joo Lee, "Dosan Ahn Chang Ho's Activities in Riverside: 1904–1914."

17. According to Sinhan Minbo's (December 19, 1913) report, Dosan registered as a new member of Los Angeles chapter in December 1913.

18. *Korean Experience Chronology in the United States* (National Institute for Korean History, 2010), 10–12.

19. Ibid; 24.

20. *Times-Picayune* (New Orleans, Louisiana), January 13, 1894: 4.

21. *San Francisco Call*, San Francisco, California. January 14, 1903: 1

22. Choy, 1979: 99.

23. Ellen Thun, *Heartwarmers*: Afterward: Change, February 25, 1997.

Chapter One

First Encounter

Analysis of the First Vision
of Ahn Chang Ho in America

"Dosan" Ahn Chang Ho came to the United States to learn English, democratic ideals, and to study Christianity in the autumn of 1902. At the time, very few Koreans lived in the United States, as large-scale official immigration did not begin until January 13, 1903. The majority of these early Koreans in America worked as ginseng merchants in California and Hawaii, and a few others were students.[1] The ginseng merchants and students clashed fiercely on ideals and cultural assimilation. Merchants showed hostility toward the students who dressed in Western style clothes and sported cropped haircuts. The Korean merchants chose not to adopt Western clothing but instead flaunted their topknots and wore their native clothes.[2] According to Yi Kang, Samuel Moffett, an American missionary, urged Dosan to accept employment with the Presbyterian church in Pyongyang (capital city of North Korea). However, Dosan declined the offer, claiming that he could serve the church just as well while supporting himself.[3] Dosan was no favorite with the missionaries. He was outspoken in his opposition to their emphasis on heavenly rewards rather than on earthly concerns and strongly asserted the primary importance of getting people to get things done here on earth.[4]

Many Americans remained completely ignorant of Korea and its customs and were unable to distinguish the peninsula from the rest of Asia. Just after Dosan and his wife arrived in San Francisco, a reporter from the *San Francisco Chronicle*, visited them at the home of Dr. Drew, a former medical missionary to Korea with whom the Ahns were staying as live-in help in East Oakland. The article may also reveal how Dosan Ahn Chang Ho became very interested in newspapers. The author noted, "I told the Coreans a little of the interesting wonders of a great American newspaper and invited them to come over some evening and let me show them all through the 'Chronicle' building and explain all the processes. The man and woman beamed their gratitude.

The Corean looked his gratefulness and said, 'I am very thankful to you. To see a great thing like that would be like giving life to a corpse.'"[5] Perhaps, this visit from the *San Francisco Chronicle* newspaper company later inspired Dosan to start the *Gongnip Sinbo* newspaper in 1905 and the *Sinhan Minbo* in 1909 as a means to inform and organize his community.

Ahn Chang Ho came to America at a time of heightened anti-Asian sentiment in California. In the early 1900s, anti-Japanese sentiment simmered in California, as demonstrated by the Asiatic Exclusion League. Developed from the Japanese and Korean Exclusion League in San Francisco in 1905, the association sought foremost to exclude Japanese immigration to the United States and secondly to segregate Asian populations from whites, especially in the school system. The *San Francisco Chronicle's* description of Ahn and his wife demonstrates the Anglo ignorance of East Asians at thetime. By highlighting the customs of the Koreans that differed from those of Anglo-Americans, the article exoticized Korea and the practices of its people. The reporter described Koreans as "devil worshipers," claimed "some households are bigger harems than those in Turkey itself," and that "one of the most noticeably peculiar things about unmarried Corean men is their close resemblance to women."[6] The reporter's impressions, informed by what Drew recounted from his eight years abroad, demonstrated the ignorance of the American public about Korea. Through its descriptions, the article also suggested Koreans' inferiority through their non-Christian religious beliefs, ways of dress, social stratification, and lack of infrastructure.

When the reporter first encountered Ahn, he took note of his western dress, as though surprised to not see him in native clothing. Even his physical description of the couple suggests an ignorance of terms in which to describe Koreans, relying instead on comparisons with other races more common in the United States: "The man was taller than the average Chinese, but looked something like a Japanese and more like some of the American Indians. The woman was under five feet and slight and looked very Japanese."[7] In addition to introducing American audiences to Korea, this article problematizes many accepted facts of Ahn Chang Ho's early days in America.

While the majority of published works on Ahn's life claim he travelled from Incheon, to Tokyo, to Honolulu, to Seattle, and then landed in San Francisco on October 14, 1902, the *San Francisco Chronicle* exposé challenges this itinerary. Instead, it confirms Do Hyung Kim's account of Dosan's itinerary that Dosan and his wife arrived in Vancouver, Canada, and later came to Seattle and finally arrived in San Francisco on October 14, 1902.[8] The article noted that Ahn and his wife boarded the incorrect ship and mistakenly arrived in Vancouver, Canada. When the two finally arrived in San Francisco, they had nearly exhausted their funds. The article further notes that Ahn and his wife accidently happened upon Dr. Drew in San Francisco's Chinatown, which proved a happy coincidence because the doctor then offered the two work as live-in help in his home in East Oakland. In his biography of Ahn, Hyung-chan Kim claims Dosan lived with Dr. Drew for more than a year.[9]

PACHAPPA CAMP: THE FIRST KOREATOWN, USA

Dosan and his wife did not stay in San Francisco long, as they relocated to Riverside, California, in 1904. Dosan first moved to Riverside on March 23, 1904. Later, his wife joined him and she gave birth to their first son, Phillip. Dosan, shortly after coming to Riverside, founded Pachappa Camp, the first Koreatown, USA. According to the autobiography of Easurk Emsen Charr, Pachappa Camp flourished.

> It had soon become the first largest Korean settlement in America, at least during the orange season of each year for a number of years. Subsequently, smaller Korean communities or camps sprung up in the nearby town of Redlands, Upland, and Claremont, which were offsprings of the main settlement which was in Riverside; before many of them began to move into the cities as operators of small shops, restaurants, and grocery stores in Los Angeles and San Francisco and in some eastern cities as they are found today.[10]

Ellen Thun sheds light on how Ahn led Korean immigrants to settle and build Pachappa Camp in Riverside. Thun said that Ahn returned from San Francisco, where he organized Koreans into forming a Friendship Association (*Chinmokhoe*), and founded Pachappa. Thun described Pachappa Camp as follows:

> It brought the scattered Koreans together, making their lives easier jobwise and their living conditions bearable. Koreans learned to help each other, to share their problems. It was a cooperative venture. Ahn Chang Ho led families to Pachappa Camp, in Riverside, California. Pachappa Camp worked successfully until the failure of orange crop in 1913, but the ten years was proof the experiment worked. Finally, *Sinhan Minbo* (October 5, 1910) report confirms that Pachappa Camp was not only the first Koreatown in America but also first location to establish local chapter of the Korean National Association of North America. Koreans lived their lifestyle, cooperatively.[11]

Although several members of Pachappa Camp, including Ahn Chang Ho's family, moved elsewhere right after the deep freeze of 1913, the camp continued to thrive and functioned as a center for the Korean immigrant community until November 1918.

There are several reasons why Dosan and his wife relocated to Riverside, California: (1) Because of the large Asian population in San Francisco, anti-Asian sentiments were very high, and it proved extremely difficult to find employment opportunities for Koreans in the area. (2) Riverside, California was one of the richest cities in the U.S. during the late nineteenth and early twentieth centuries, with plenty of employment opportunities in the thriving citrus industry. (3) Several friends of Dosan, including Yi Kang and Chung Chae Kwan, were already working on citrus farms in Riverside, California, and they urged him to join them in the south.[12] According to testimony Ahn delivered before a Japanese judge later on in his life, he also claimed to have moved south for a more hospitable climate.[13]

CITRUS INDUSTRY AND RIVERSIDE

"The City of Riverside was founded in 1870 by John North and a group of Easterners who wished to establish a colony dedicated to furthering education and culture. Investors from England and Canada transplanted traditions and activities adopted by prosperous citizens; the first golf course and polo field in Southern California were built in Riverside."[14] In 1885, Riverside was being acclaimed as the "Home of the Naval Orange."[15] With the completion of the Gage Canal in November 1886, land value increased from $1 an acre to $25.[16] By 1900, citrus fruit production had an impact on every Riverside household. Riverside packinghouses employed more than 1,200 men as pickers, packers, and bookkeepers.[17] Riverside became one of the richest cities in the United States with plenty of job opportunities by the early 1900s.[18] Fairmont Park built in 1880 was praised as one of the greatest parks in the world.[19] Ten former presidents of the United States visited the Glenwood Mission Inn Resort and Spa located in downtown Riverside. Richard Nixon was married at the Mission Inn Hotel and Spa in 1940 as well.

Dosan Ahn Chang Ho came to Riverside to work and make a living in the thriving citrus industry that offered plenty of employment opportunities. When he established the Korean Labor Bureau sometime between 1904 and 1905, Pachappa Camp became the center of the Korean immigrant community. Bong-youn Choy describes how Korean immigrants secured orange picking jobs in Riverside, California.

Perhaps it might be worth telling the story of how Koreans were able to secure orange-picking jobs on Riverside farms, which the American orchard owners preferred Orientals to white laborers. The wages of the Orientals were lower but they produced more work. They were willing to work longer hours without overtime pay, and they obeyed the instructions of the employer without any complaints. At this period, orange-picking was more or less monopolized by the Japanese. Therefore, the members of the *Gongnip Hyophoe* worked out detailed plans for securing orange-picking jobs in competition with the Japanese.[20]

Ahn Chang Ho and the *Gongnip Hyophoe* established a plan to relocate newly arriving Korean immigrants from Korea and Hawaii to Riverside, California. Bong-youn Choy explained the plan:

Physically strong and experienced Koreans were to be sent to the Riverside orchards as a sample labor force. They were told to construct their own living quarters as soon as they arrived, without asking for any money from the Americans. Then they were to organize a working team of ten men. Each man on the team was supposed to follow these working guidelines: "Our only capital today in this land is nothing but honesty; therefore, work diligently without wasting time whether your employer watches you or not; then you will be working not only today but tomorrow and even the whole year around. If your employer has confidence in you, then your friends, Kim, Lee, or Park will also get jobs, because of your hard and honest work. In this way, eventually all Koreans will get jobs anywhere and at any time."[21]

Choy (1979) continues that "with these instructions, the newcomers were sent out to the Riverside orchard farms. Most of them did not have money and did not speak English. So, the members of the *Gongnip Hyophoe* collected money and bought train tickets for their fellow Koreans. They also prepared lunch boxes. When the working team got on the train, the leaders of the *Gongnip Hyophoe* told the conductor the name of the station where they were to get off." In other words, the *Gongnip Hyophoe* and Dosan Ahn Chang Ho devised a plan to settle Korean immigrants in Riverside and executed it accordingly. As a result of the carefully devised plan to settle Korean immigrants in Riverside, the number of Korean settlers in Riverside grew rapidly.

According to the *Gongnip Sinbo* (December 21, 1905), the number of *Gongnip Hyophoe* members in Riverside was seventy as of November 1905. This number does not include women and children. As of June 1907, the number of *Gongnip Hyophoe* members at Pachappa Camp increased to 150.[22] If we include the number of women and children as well as temporary fruit pickers during the orange picking season, more than three hundred Koreans resided at Pachappa Camp during the peak season. According to the *Gongnip Sinbo* (December 6, 1905), In Soo Kim, a Korean labor contractor, was looking for one hundred workers to pick oranges in Riverside. Many Korean immigrants in Hawaii feared that they would not be able to migrate to mainland United States if the "Gentleman's Agreement" took effect. The Gentleman's Agreement of 1907 prohibited migration of Japanese immigrants to the United States mainland. As "Japanese subjects," Korean immigrants feared that they would be limited by the agreement. Thus, several hundred Koreans from Hawaii decided to relocate to San Francisco before 1907. (Japan made Korea a protectorate in 1905 and thus, Koreans were considered Japanese subjects. Japan formally occupied the Korean peninsula in 1910.)

PACHAPPA CAMP: THE FIRST KOREATOWN IN THE UNITED STATES

As the number of Korean immigrants grew, Pachappa Camp became the focal point of the early Korean immigrant community and the center of its independence movement in America. There are several reasons why Pachappa Camp should be known as the first Koreatown in the United States of America: (1) Unlike other places, Pachappa Camp housed families including women and children, (2) Dosan's leadership, and his rules, regulations, and guidelines for the community—Dosan's Republic—gave it organizational structure. Also, under Dosan's leadership, the community functioned with democratic principles and operated as an autonomously governed community (3) the Korean Labor Bureau also provided employment opportunities, administrative and economic structure that residents could rely upon (4) independence organizations like the *Gongnip Hyophoe*, the *Shinminhoe*, and the Korean National Association of North America Riverside chapter, held meetings and activities including lectures and fundraising at the camp, (5) residents constructed a central dining hall where they held community and cultural activities such as wedding receptions, birthday parties, Sunday services, and more, (6) the community also had a Korean Mission and one of the camp's residents, Soon Hak Kim, later became pastor. The mission was supported by the local Calvary Presbyterian Church of Riverside. English classes and services were held at the mission which was located at the camp, and (7) Pachappa Camp residents played a critical role in gaining recognition by the U.S. government of Korean identity and rejecting the "Japanese subject" label.

An article published on October 5, 1910, by the Korean newspaper *Sinhan Minbo,* corroborates that Riverside is the first Koreatown in America. "Pachappa Camp is the first *Dong-nae* (organized-Korean American settlement) and the first Korean National Association local chapter was established in the United States." The *Sinhan Minbo* article also reported that "members of the Riverside KNA chapter frequently relocated for work, and at times it was uncertain if they could remain at Pachappa Camp. However, Mr. In Soo Kim and his family, who settled in Riverside, helped negotiate rental fees and paid for those who could not afford rent and provided leadership therefore helping to maintain a cohesive community."[23] Mr. In Soo Kim was Helen Ahn's distant relative, and he played an important role shaping the early period of Pachappa Camp in the absence of Dosan Ahn Chang Ho between 1907 and 1911. Easurk Emsen Charr also named the Riverside Korean community as the "first and largest Korean settlement in America." In his autobiography, Charr wrote:

> Down in the sunny Southland in those balmy spring days in Riverside, I was happy now that my cousin and his wife were with me again. They liked the place, the climate, the work, and the living conditions here as I did and the others, too. No wonder it had soon become the first largest Korean settlement in America, at least during the orange season of each year for a number of years. Subsequently, smaller nearby towns of Redlands, Upland, and Claremont, which were offsprings of the main settlement which was in Riverside: that is, before many of them began to move into the cities as operators of small shops, restaurants, and grocery stores in Los Angeles and San Francisco and in some eastern cities as they are found today.[24]

It is important to note that Charr also confirms that Riverside was the first and largest Korean settlement in the United States before Korean immigrants relocated to large cities such as Los Angeles and San Francisco. Sunju Lee who proposed the idea of Pachappa Camp as the first Koreatown in the United States estimated the number of Korean residents to be around sixty-five to seventy.[25] But as mentioned above, the number of Korean residents could have been as large as three hundred or more during the orange picking season (December to February).

On January 31, 1918, the *Sinhan Minbo* reported the closure of the Riverside Chapter of the Korean National Association of North America:

> Commemorative Riverside Chapter [at] 1532 Pachappa Avenue is the location of Riverside Chapter of Korean National Association of North America. It is the birthplace of the Korean National Association of North America. All members of Korean National Association of North America show respect and love toward Riverside Chapter but recently we received regrettable news. According to report from Riverside chapter, the total number of Riverside chapter is forty-five that include fifteen adults, ten wives, and twenty children. However, only 1/9 pays dues and four or five attend meetings. Only fifteen attends church services including children. Therefore, Riverside chapter is unable to sustain itself and decided to shut down this month. Los Angeles chapter also decided to shut down but later reversed to maintain its chapter. Hopefully, Riverside chapter can reverse its decision and maintain chapter. Riverside chapter has the longer history and made more contribution than Los Angeles.

The *Sinhan Minbo* report made clear that the Riverside KNA chapter had a longer history and played more important roles in the independence movement than the Los Angeles chapter. The fact that the *Sinhan Minbo* used terms such as "Historic" and "Commemorative" to describe Pachappa Camp and the Riverside Chapter of the Korean National Association of North America confirms and corroborates that Pachappa Camp is the first Koreatown in America. Indeed, Pachappa Camp was not only the first Koreatown in America but also the center of early Korean community and independence movement activities during the early twentieth century.

The Korean settlement at Pachappa also included political exiles who escaped from Japanese oppression immediately after the assassination of Prince Itō Hirobumi. Ito was a politician and Prime Minister of Japan. He was killed on October 29, 1909, in China at the Harbin Railway Station by Korean independence activist An Jung-geun.

> Fortunately the report from Korea told how the court trying Chung-kun Ahn had decided there had been no conspiracy in Prince Ito's death and ordered the leaders released, that the assassin had acted alone. This news was followed by Korean refugees and asylum seekers appearing in Riverside. They said they were escaping while they had a chance; they were mostly, students. Their stories inflamed the Pachappa camp residents even more than before.[26]

Many of the Koreans who came to the U.S. mainland found employment opportunities in Riverside as largely migrant farm workers. Koreans worked "school-boy jobs" that included cooking and cleaning for families, and they also found positions in hospitality. Upon his arrival, Dosan had little difficulty finding work as a domestic helper, and he began cooking for an affluent Riverside family. The word about the plentiful jobs spread quickly among Koreans in nearby communities and more Koreans came to Riverside.[27] With the establishment of the Korean Labor Bureau, Ahn ensured the employment of Korean immigrants and the growth of the Korean population in Riverside.

PACHAPPA CAMP AND THE KOREAN LABOR BUREAU

In Riverside, CA, Pachappa Camp grew around the Korean Labor Bureau (1904 or 1905), which aided Koreans in finding jobs primarily in agriculture in the region. With work readily available, Pachappa Camp became the center of early Korean settlement in the United States—the first Koreatown, USA. White owners of citrus farms, including Cornelius E. Rumsey, in Riverside preferred to hire Korean laborers as they worked diligently and production increased to their satisfaction. According to the *Gongnip Sinbo* (April 14, 1906: 2), Japanese laborers confronted Korean laborers for taking jobs away from them.

Japanese laborers dominated labor force in Riverside. Two years ago, Korean immigrants began to arrive and work in Riverside. Ranchers preferred to hire Korean workers and only hired Japanese laborers if additional workers were needed. Japanese workers asked to ranchers why do you prefer hiring Korean workers over Japanese laborers? Ranchers responded that Korean workers are diligent and hard workers. Japanese workers did not know what to say to ranchers. Japanese laborers came to see Korean labor contractor and asked, 'Why do you take jobs away from us?' Korean labor contractor responded that we are not taking jobs away from you, but we work hard as instructed by ranchers.

The Korean Labor Bureau (KLB) was likely established in mid-to-late 1904. The *Gongnip Sinbo* report suggests that Korean workers in Riverside worked hard and diligently as instructed by Ahn Chang Ho and gained trust from white ranchers and farmers. In fact, a 1906 *Gongnip Sinbo* article reported that the KLB might have been already established in 1904, as Korean labor contractors had already been placing workers since that year.[28]

Dosan Ahn Chang Ho played a pivotal role in establishing the Korean Labor Bureau. Soon after settling in Riverside, Ahn became acquainted with Cornelius Earle Rumsey, a wealthy resident of Riverside and owner of Alta Cresta Groves, a citrus farm near Pachappa Camp. Rumsey suggested to Ahn that he and other Koreans go to work in his orchards in 1904, and the offer opened up fruit picking for Koreans in Riverside.[29] Previously, Koreans had faced several impediments to working in agriculture, as Japanese labor contractors held a monopoly on fruit picking. Ranchers and farmers went through labor bureaus to hire workers, and the Japanese labor contractors in the region would only contract jobs to other Japanese immigrants. Despite the plethora of positions available picking and packing fruit in Riverside, without their own labor bureau, Koreans found it difficult to gain contracts to work in the orchards.[30]

Rumsey understood Ahn's predicament and suggested the Koreans in the city come work at his orchard. In addition, Rumsey loaned Ahn fifteen hundred dollars. A conversation mentioned in *Willow Tree Shade* describes how the Korean Labor Bureau was established. "Sasaki gives work only to the Japanese workers, not us. Labor contractor, Sasaki would not place Korean workers to ranchers." Most labor contractors were Japanese at the time and they discriminated against Korean workers. "The landlord asked, 'Why don't you set up a hiring hall yourself?' Someone answered, 'We would need money for setting up the office, and we don't have any money for that.' Landlord asked, 'How much money do you need?' Someone replied, 'We need about $1,500 to $1,600.' That night the landlord agreed to front $1,500 for a hiring office stating, 'I don't expect any interest on the money, and I will talk to the newspaper for advertising and the telephone company. I wish you the best.'"[31]

With the money, Dosan could lease housing and office space to start an employment agency designed to serve Korean workers.[32] In March 1905, the Korean Employment Bureau operated from 127 Cottage Street (today 3065 Cottage Street)[33], but by October of the same year, the Korean Labor Bureau had moved into a larger building across the street at 1532 Pachappa Avenue.[34] The job opportunities flourished, and a March advertisement in the *Riverside Daily News* ran: "Korean Employment Bureau Orange Pickers, domestic help and laborers furnished on short notice." In October 20, 1905, another *Riverside Daily News* advertisement appeared with new phrases: "All kind of help furnished on short notice—orange pickers, house cleaners and gardeners. Give us a trial and we will convince you that we are not afraid to work." O. Kim was listed as the contact person for the advertisement placed by the Korean Labor Bureau. The advertisement also listed a telephone number for the KLB as Sunset Phone Red 3677. Despite the Korean workers' low wages, the residents saved their money and repaid Rumsey after only a month and a half. According to *Willow Tree Shade*, "they were so busy that they had to put in a second telephone in one month. They paid off the $1,500 loan as well."[35] Riverside's labor bureau and Koreatown proved a strong drawing force for immigrants. They knew they could find work easily with the systems in place and the camp helped reunite families and friends, even further increasing its import to the Korean community in America.[36]

Nin (pronounced In) Soo Kim, distant relative of Helen Ahn, also served as a labor contractor for the Korean Labor Bureau in 1905. He and his son, Yong Nun, moved to Riverside in 1904. In Soo Kim stated that he had been a resident of Riverside for sixteen years in his application to move to Hawaii in 1920. (In fact, Yong Nun Kim's children never left Riverside, and the youngest daughter Catherine Violet Kim passed away on April 23, 2018, in Riverside. Her death marked the end of an era). In Soo Kim was an integral part of Pachappa Camp and helped Dosan Ahn Chang Ho operate the Korean community during the early 1900s.

At the same time, Ahn encouraged Korean workers in Riverside to pick oranges as if they were their own and promoted independence movement activities. He told his fellow countrymen to work diligently and honestly because such efforts contributed to the freedom of Korea. "When you pick an orange, you pick it for your homeland; when you clean a toilet, you do it for your country! When we pick one orange, we must pick that orange as if our country's future depends on it."[37] Pachappa Korean workers became the favorite among ranchers because they brought the best-looking fruits and recorded the least amount of spoilage.[38] Under Dosan Ahn Chang Ho's leadership, Pachappa Camp workers gained the trust and understanding from ranch owners. Pachappa Camp residents also helped find employment opportunities for newly arriving Korean immigrant workers at the orchards.

Ellen Thun, who was born in Riverside in 1912 and documented the lives of the Koreans there, described the relationship between grove owners and Korean workers in Riverside.

> The orange grove owner invited the Korean workers and their families to a dinner at the church. Their relationship had been a good one for several reasons. Still, the Koreans had to wonder. Whoever in all of Riverside had heard of such an event? Invited by the American owner to sup with him. Biblical! No, the owner told them it was because his groves had shown a profit every year since they had picked oranges for him. Now he wanted to thank them. The dinner was a success and the minister of the church arose from his chair and gave each man a Bible and hymnbook. Mr. Ahn, sitting at the host's table, was seen to smile widely. (He was not known to smile widely.) Mrs. Ahn caught his eye from where she sat and returned her own special look. It meant, You have won your point.[39]

Susan Ahn described what was said at the same event.

> I have been watching the Korean workers for the past year, and I am pleasantly surprised and thankful for how wonderful you all are. I have checked with the post office and they tell me that a lot of you send money home regularly. At the bank they tell me that you save most of your earnings and some of you use checks in your business dealings. There aren't any Koreans in the shady parts of Chinatown. Americans could learn a lot of things from you. I would be even happier if you could get rid of the smoking habit.[40]

Ranchers were impressed by how hard Korean workers picked oranges and were happy because profits increased. Therefore, ranchers were willing to hire Korean workers, and Pachappa Camp became the favorite destination of Korean immigrant workers. In addition, ranchers hired Korean and other Asian immigrant workers because wages for them were lower, they worked longer hours, and produced more crops and thus, profit. During orange picking season, the number of Korean laborers increased. The season typically began right before Christmas and lasted for about ten weeks. Bong-youn Choy also tells the story of how Korean immigrants were able to secure orange-picking jobs on Riverside farms.

> The plan was as follows. Physically strong and experienced Koreans were to be sent to the Riverside orchards as a sample labor force. They were told to construct their own living quarters as soon as they arrived, without asking for any

money from the Americans. Then they were to organize a working team of ten men. Each man on the team was supposed to follow these working guidelines.[41]

The working guidelines were written by Ahn Chang Ho and issued in the name of the *Gongnip Hyophoe*, according to Yang Choo-en, the Reverend Whang Sa-sun, and other early immigrants.[42]

In late 1904 or early 1905, the number of Koreans in Riverside began to increase, and to encourage cohesion among the group, Ahn suggested finding a larger residence to accommodate Riverside's growing Korean population. Koreans in Riverside rented barracks, once used by Chinese Americans to build the railroads, at 1532 Pachappa Avenue and moved into the run-down shacks, thus establishing the first organized Korean settlement or Koreatown on the United States.[43] Never before had Koreans lived in one organized neighborhood in the continental United States. One resident of the community, Mary Paik Lee, described the poor living conditions of Pachappa Camp in her memoir:

> We lived in a small one-room shack built in the 1880s. The passing of time had made the lumber shrink, so the wind blew through the cracks in the walls. There was no pretense of making it livable—just four walls, one window, and one door—nothing else. We put mud in the cracks to keep the wind out. The water pump served several shacks. We had to heat our bath water in a bucket over an open fire outside, then pour it into a tin tub inside. There was no gas or electricity. We used kerosene lamps, and one of my chores was to trim the wicks, clean the glass tops, and keep the bowls filled with kerosene.[44]

Jacob Thun (also spelled Dunn), left an unpublished manuscript about his life. He was the cousin of Ellen Thun and was a well-known Korean for his independence activities and more. Jacob Thun recalled his early life in Riverside vividly in his manuscript which he gave to his cousin. Ellen noted in the margins of the manuscript that "What remains of his image is the young boy who was unfailingly good-humored in his uncle's overcrowded household where there were never enough beds, so the boys slept four-in-one sometimes and often on the floor."[45] Jacob described his early high school days in Riverside and stated that "there was no high school except in the town of Riverside. [I] walked, with Frank, about five or six miles each way." Frank is Jacob's older brother who came to Riverside in 1907 from Hawaii to live with their uncle, Nak Chung Thun.[46] Jacob also described the poor living conditions of Pachappa Camp, "The floors of the frame shack they occupied had cracks, as well as splinters. There was no cash left from paying bills, so the floors were bare. She (Nak Chung's wife) wished she could weave mats, but she had no time, and this was a moment she wished her sister-in-law, Jacob's and Frank's mother, were with her."[47]

Jacob and Franks's mother and father were living in Hawaii at the time. Frank and Jacob also recalled their first encounter with Dosan Ahn Chang Ho in Oakland before Ahn left for Korea in 1907.

> Frank and Jacob knew this was a great moment of their lives when Mr. Ahn shook their hands and spoke directly to them. He said, 'I am a laborer and I work for Korea. Korea's freedom is life's greatest cause. And for this reason you have come. For this reason I go there now.' They shook his hands and were proud, although they did not understand his words entirely, but they knew he was opposing the Japanese and arousing their own countrymen to fight for independence. Nara-il![48]

PACHAPPA'S HISTORICAL SIGNIFICANCE IN KOREAN IMMIGRATION

Large-scale official Korean immigration opened to the United States in 1903, when Hawaiian sugar planters contracted Koreans to work in their fields through the intermediary David Deshler. "Deshler arranged for the Hawaiian Sugar Planters Association to front him capital to pay the Koreans' passage to the islands from Asia, a common practice made illegal when Hawaii became a territory of the United States in 1898."[49] Deshler enticed workers with the promise of money growing on trees, island living, and laid back work. He also illegally had them sign two-year contracts abroad to work on sugar or pineapple plantations; United States law permitted signing such contracts only on U.S. soil. Deshler deliberately deceived the Korean immigrants, who discovered upon their arrival the terrible conditions on sugar plantations and the pitiful remittance they received. Since they signed two-year contracts before immigrating, the planters required them to see out their duties, and because of this reason, it was not until 1905 when workers' contracts expired that any large number of Koreans began moving to the United States mainland.[50] Railroad and California fruit representatives had travelled to Hawaii offering plantation laborers higher wages for less grueling work, and hundreds of Koreans consequently flocked to the golden state. At this time, Koreans began arriving in Riverside from Hawaii and Dosan Ahn Chang Ho worked alongside individuals such as Im Chun-gi to find work for these Koreans. The growth of Pachappa Camp therefore reflects patterns of Korean immigration to the United States, as few Koreans lived in California prior to 1905. Not until that time did enough Koreans settle on the mainland to enable communal living.

Riverside proved a popular location for Koreans because of the work available and the Koreatown in place. Families moved to Riverside constantly to earn a steady living, support friends and relatives, and to seek education. In 1907, Ellen Thun's parents also came from Hawaii, along with several others, via San Francisco to Riverside in search of higher pay and educating their children.

> The Chuns had only the clothes they had brought with them from Hawaii, which they now layered onto themselves; thus clad, they made their entry into Riverside and went in search of Pachapa Camp. There was no difficulty finding the camp. It was located in bare countryside, flanked on either side by the Santa Fe line and the Union Pacific. A dirt road, called Pachapa Street, led along the rail lines and behold, there was the camp.[51]

In the early 1900s, another uncle of Helen Ahn's, N. Kim, held the position as camp boss at Dosan's Republic. Kim had followed his family to America and inland to Riverside for work as head of the labor bureau in its early years.[52] Another example of Riverside's role in reuniting families and friends comes from Easurk Emsen Charr, an acquaintance of Ahn's from Korea. He followed Dosan to Riverside with the Shinn family just before the orange harvest in 1905. Charr had travelled from Hawaii to San Francisco with the Shinns, and they had worked together picking grapes around Fresno before heading south in the fall. When they reached Riverside, the group found another of their steerage companions from their Hawaiian voyage, D. Y. Oh. Thus, Riverside stood as an important leg of many Koreans' migrations within the United States. The next spring, Charr's cousin Chungsurk and his wife joined them in Riverside. Charr eventually moved away to attend university in Missouri, but later returned to Riverside and worked as a waiter at the Glenwood Hotel, later known as the Mission Inn.[53] Another family, the Paiks, came to Riverside in December 1906 to likewise meet families from their village outside of Pyongyang. They stayed in Riverside a number of years to earn money, and eventually moved to central California to begin sharecropping.

COMMUNITY AT PACHAPPA

Although the Chinese workers who constructed the Santa Fe Railroad in the late 1880s originally built and inhabited the barracks that came to be known as Pachappa Camp, Koreans were the first ethnic community to build cultural capital on the site.[54] Ellen Thun described Pachappa Camp in her writings:

> The camp held about 20 small houses, all painted red and identically alike. These structures were built for the Union Pacific workers many years before and abandoned when the rail tracks were completed. Since then, migrant work-

ers made the camp their headquarters, with the Koreans' arrival of recent date: 1904. The Chuns saw a Korean sign which read "Korean Labor Bureau" and they knew they were home. A gentleman came out of the house with the sign on it and said he had expected them earlier for the general meeting of the association. He said he was the owner of the sign, as well as the general manager, at the moment, of Pachappa camp. He said to follow him, he would get them settled. They were shown a three-room house, with beds—No more sleeping on straws! And a kerosene stove and lamp. A kitchen of sorts, with a table holding pots, pans, dishes, and beside one table leg, a sack of rice! Also a small glass jar of kimchi. Mrs. Chun had to turn away her face to hide the tears beginning to well up in her eyes. How kind! Familiar halmoni faces welled up with the tears—each one the kindly face of one she had known long ago.[55]

When asked later about Pachappa Camp during a videotaped interview, Ellen Thun recalled Pachappa Camp with more detail. She discussed the grounds of the site, what was there, and even remembers the types of trees that dotted the landscape of the area.

I think the thing about Camp Pachappa that stays with most of us is the fact that there were pepper trees all over the grounds. They looked so dreary because Riverside was always hot and dusty and the trees just sort of limped and the red berries were always falling off. It wasn't a beautiful sight, but we remember the pepper tree at Pachappa Camp the best, I think, because all those I interviewed later on they said, "Oh yes, the pepper trees," and my cousin who was writing his story about Pachappa mentioned the pepper trees. Then of course there were eucalyptus trees and California oaks. But aside from that the grounds were very dusty and rocky and not at all pretty as you would think a city should have, you know, grass and stuff. But the families did use the grounds to plant a little bit of lettuce and onions, things like that.[56]

At the settlement, Koreans fostered a strong sense of community through their shared lifestyles. While men worked on farms, women also participated in the everyday functions of the camp, cooking and cleaning for manual laborers. In its early days, men headed to Riverside's dump yard to salvage scraps with which they built a dining hall to contain a long table and benches to seat the workers so they could all eat together. One of the residents, Paik Sin Koo, built an oven from mud and straw to serve the families, and one woman, Son Kuang Do, cooked three meals a day for about thirty men when she lived in Riverside in 1906.[57] Workers in Riverside's orchards picked oranges, lemons, and grapefruits in the winter. In the summer, they picked deciduous fruits in the surrounding areas, such as peaches and apricots, and in the fall, they harvested walnuts. During orange season, many Korean workers came to Riverside to work and meet old friends.

As soon as the grape season was over, the Shinn family and I left for Riverside where the orange season would come next in about ten weeks, a little before the Christmas season. I was glad to be in Riverside where there were many old friends of mine who went before me, including my pal, Oh, and Mr. Ahn Chang-ho himself, his wife and her uncle, N. Kim, the camp boss and the best-known Korean in Riverside.[58]

Women typically worked in packinghouses during citrus season and, along with children, helped to gather and hull nuts the men shook from the trees in autumn. Some Koreans found work as domestics for wealthy families while others worked at businesses in Riverside such as hotels, hospitals, and cement companies.[59] Ellen Thun talked about how Korean immigrants did whatever was necessary to survive economically.

Mrs. Chun had learned to use a sewing machine in Kauai, one had been available at the mission house. Although she learned how to sew with needle and thread and had made all her clothes by hand, she now wanted to make clothes with a sewing machine. She asked her husband, if you come across a sewing machine that someone discards, Yobo, perhaps you could offer two or three dollars for it? If it needs repair, young Mr. Park will know how to do it, and he won't charge too much.[60]

Mr. Chun soon got one in exchange for gardening service he provided to a lady. She asked, "Could your wife use an old Singer?" Mr. Chun took the sewing machine home in a borrowed wheelbarrow. Now, Mrs. Chun was ready to sew, and the first thing or things were trousers for the boys; they were britches with buckles at the knees.[61]

Unfortunately, Mrs. Thun attempted suicide a few months after the March 1 movement in Korea and was hospitalized. Her five youngest children, under nine years of age, were placed in the Riverside County Children's Home, an orphanage.[62] In 1921, Mr. Chun was asked to plant grapevines in Imperial County by local real estate developers. Mr. Chun took up this offer and relocated to Imperial County and planted fifteen thousand grapevines.[63] He left his children in Riverside.

INTERETHNIC RELATIONS

At the turn of the twentieth century, Riverside was home to a diverse population, and the Korean community relied on the help of established residents to develop its settlement and enrich the lives of its community. Before Koreans came to Riverside, the city already hosted a well-established Chinatown. In order to stock their residences, new arrivals, such as Paik Sin Koo, communicated with Chinese merchants using *hanja*, the classical Chinese *hanmun* script common to Chinese and Korean. Using the writing, Paik borrowed household materials and food on credit.[64] Ellen Thun also recalls children frequently walked to the Chinese store where they would buy ice cream cones.[65] In addition to their collaboration with other minorities, the Korean community also integrated to an extent with Riverside's white population. Members of the Presbyterian Church in Riverside came to the settlement to give English lessons. Cornelius E. Rumsey also reportedly allowed the use of his house for church services and English classes for his Korean workers. One resident Easurk Emsen Charr recalled meeting a shoe-salesman with whom he became acquainted because the clerk corrected his English. The two then attended Presbyterian Church services together and the salesman later employed Charr to perform some housework.[66]

The Ladies Society invited Korean women to their meetings to talk about Korean culture and exchange ideas. Mary Paik Lee and Helen Lee Hong recalled one lady, Mrs. Stewart from Upland, who came to their church on Sundays and brought children presents on Christmas. Christianity consequently proved a productive shoe-in to learning English and forging transcultural bonds.[67] As individuals became better established in the city, they also participated in larger projects to benefit the city. According to a *Riverside Enterprise* article, entitled "Korean Residents Give To Fund For Local Hospital," one resident named Nak Sun Park (who was identified as C. S. Park in the article), a soldier at March Air Field, offered $53 collected from four Korean families to the chairman of the hospital building commission, Ross Hammond.[68] Park later joined the Willows Korean Aviation School in 1920, a flight school developed in Northern California in order to train Korean aviators to fight in armed combat to regain their country's independence from Japan.[69]

While pursuing education, dawning Western clothes, and converting to Christianity eased transition to American life, many Koreans still experienced prejudice from their neighbors. Korean workers received lower wages than workers of European descent, they could not access white-collar professions, and they often experienced different forms of hostility from whites. While attending elementary school in Riverside, Mary Paik Lee recalled how students sang "Ching Chong Chinaman, Sitting on a wall. Along came a white man, And chopped his head off," tapping her on the neck at the end of the song to mime her decapitation.[70] The *Riverside Daily Press* (January 6, 1906) reported an anti-Korean hate crime with the title "Villainous Spite Work."

One of the most despicable bits of criminal spite work which has come to light for some time was uncovered this morning, when five Korean boys brought their bicycles [to] Bryan Bros shop with the tires literally slashed to pieces. The tires on the five wheels were worth fully $35, and they have been cut beyond possible repair with great knife gashes. It was evidently work of some sneaking hobo with an imaginary wrong against Koreans and Japanese, or some low-minded orange picker out of job for some cause or another. The Koreans are working for F. D. Lewis on the F. M. Tutin ranch."

Discrimination also proved institutional. On March 14, 1907, President Theodore Roosevelt passed Executive Order 589, expressly prohibiting secondary migration of Korean and Japanese laborers from Hawaii, Mexico, and Canada to the continental United States in order to maintain mainland and island labor conditions. Following this executive order, only picture brides, students and political exiles could travel to the mainland until 1945. Thus, Koreans' physical movement from Hawaii to the mainland faced restrictions. After the California state legislature passed the Alien Land Law on March 19, 1913, Korean Americans could not own land or hold long-term leases in the state.[71] Such legal limits to Koreans' freedom to move and work further restricted their abilities to amass wealth and advance their social status.

Yet, Pachappa Camp, which housed men, women, children, and families, thrived under Dosan Ahn Chang Ho's leadership and democratic principals. With plenty of employment opportunities in Riverside, Korean immigrants came and settled at Pachappa Camp and it became the first Koreatown, USA. Despite poverty and hardship, Pachappa Koreans never forgot about the plight of their homeland, which was in the process of being colonized by Japan. Pachappa Camp Korean immigrants mobilized its financial and human resources to fight for the independence of Korea, and it became the center of early Korean independence movement activities in the United States.

NOTES

1. See Wayne Patterson, *From the Land of Hibiscus: Koreans in Hawai'i, 1903–1950* (Honolulu: University of Hawaii Press, 2007).

2. Arthur Leslie Gardner, The Korean Nationalist Movement and An Chang-Ho, Advocate of Gradualism. Ph.D. dissertation, University of Hawaii, 1979: 30.

3. Ibid, 25.

4. Ibid, quoted from *DongA Ilbo*, March 19, 1963.

5. *San Francisco Chronicle, "Corea: The Sleeping Land"* December 7, 1902: 11.

6. Ibid.

7. Ibid.

8. Do Hyung Kim, "Dosan Ahn Chang Ho's Independence Activities through his Passport" 37th The Dosan Society conference.

9. Hyung-chan Kim,1996: 31.

10. Charr, Easurk Emsen, *The Golden Mountain: The Autobiography of a Korean Immigrant: 1895–1960.* University of Illinois Press, 1961: 153.

11. Ellen Thun, "Today's Summit Meeting; Yesterday's Pyongyang." Korea Times. August 14, 2000. Ellen Thun was born in Riverside and grew up in orphanage and worked for room and board as a domestic. She wrote every chance she had and left a collection of "heartwarmers"—delightful and insightful sketches of Korean life in Riverside. It was published by Korea Times between 1994 and 2000.

12. Sunju Lee, "Dosan Ahn Chang Ho's Activities in Riverside: 1904–1914," in *The Independence Movement and its Outgrowth by Korean Americans* (Los Angeles: Centennial Committee of Korean Immigration to the U.S., 2003), 111–192; Hyung Chan Kim, *Tosan Ahn Ch'ang Ho: A Profile of a Prophetic Patriot* (Seoul: Tosan Memorial Foundation, 1996), 132–135.

13. Kim, *Tosan Ahn Ch'ang Ho,* 32.

14. Calvary Presbyterian Church 125th Anniversary Celebration Worship Heritage Sunday June 24, 2012.

15. Joan H. Hall, *A Citrus Legacy. Riverside, California.* Highgrove Press, 1992: 23.

16. *Ibid,* 32.

17. *Ibid.,* 79.

18. Joan H. Hall, *A Citrus Legacy. Riverside, California*: Highgrove Press, 1992.

19. Patricia Stewart, *Fairmont Park: Riverside's Treasure.* Riverside, Ca: 2005.

20. Bong-youn Choy, *Koreans in America.* Chicago: Nelson Hall Press, 1979: 106.

21. According to several Korean immigrants including Yang Ju Eun and Hwang Sa-sun, these rules were written by Dosan Ahn Chang Ho.

22. *Gongnip Sinbo,* December 21, 1905.

23. In Soo Kim is Helen Ahn's uncle. Although In Soo Kim is his Korean name, his English spelling is Nin Soo Kim.

24. Easurk Emsen Charr, *The Golden Mountain: The Autobiography of a Korean Immigrant 1895–1960.* Urbana and Chicago: University of Illinois Press, 1961: 153.

25. Sunju Lee, "Dosan Ahn Chang Ho's Activities in Riverside: 1904–1914," in *The Independence Movement and its Outgrowth by Korean Americans* (Los Angeles: Centennial Committee of Korean Immigration to the U.S., 2003), 111–192; Hyung Chan Kim, *Tosan Ahn Ch'ang Ho: A Profile of a Prophetic Patriot* (Seoul: Tosan Memorial Foundation, 1996), 135

26. Ellen Thun, "Heartwarmers: Annexation," *Korea Times.* January 28, 1997.

27. John Cha, Willow Tree Shade: The Susan Ahn Cuddy Story. Korean American Heritage Foundation, 2002: 40.

28. *Gongnip Sinbo,* April 14, 1906: 12.

29. How Ahn and Rumsey first became acquainted remains unclear. Some scholars such as Vince Moses speculate they became acquainted through church involvement, while other more anecdotal sources such as Byung-il Kim's work *Korean American Pioneer Dosan-A Biography of Dosan Chang-Ho Ahn* tells a story of the two meeting as Ahn rested under a tree one afternoon and Rumsey walked by and started a conversation. Tom Patterson, "Early Riverside dotted by housing for farm workers," *Press Enterprise,* October 1, 1989, B-5.

30. See Cletus E. Daniel, *Bitter Harvest: A History of California Farmworkers, 1870–1941* (Ithaca and London: Cornell University Press), 74.

31. John Cha, Willow Tree Shade: The Susan Ahn Cuddy Story. Korean American Heritage Foundation, 2002: 40.

32. Vince Moses, "Oranges and Independence: Cornelius Earle Rumsey and Ahn Chang Ho; An Early East-West Alliance in Riverside, 1904–1911," *Riverside Museum Associates News Letter,* June 2000.

33. *Riverside Daily Press*, March 22, 1905: 8.

34. *Riverside Daily Press*, October 20, 1905: 8

35. John Cha, Willow Tree Shade: The Susan Ahn Cuddy Story. Korean American Heritage Foundation, 2002: 40.

36. Mary Paik Lee, *Quiet Odyssey: A Pioneer Korean Women in America* (Seattle: University of Washington Press, 1990).

37. *Ibid*, 2002: 39.

38. *Ibid*, 2002: 39–40.

39. Ellen Thun, "Heartwarmers" Korea Times. February 1, 1995: 3.

40. John Chan, 2002: 41.

41. Choy, 1979: 106.

42. *Ibid*, footnote 1 in chapter 6.

43. Kim, *Tosan Ahn Ch'ang-Ho,* 34. The precise date of the establishment of the camp remains unknown, although the block at Cottage and Pachappa became clearly established as a Korean settlement by 1905. It remains unclear if the Koreans residing in Riverside before Ahn arrived already lived at that location, or if his loan provided the capital for them to move.

44. Mary Paik Lee, *Quiet Odyssey*. Seattle: University of Washington Press, 1990:15.

45. An unpublished manuscript was given to Edward T. Chang in 1993 during interview with Ellen Thun. Inside of manuscript, I found a Personal Note: A Sketch of JJ's character (seen from my view) Temporary title: Cousin Rose A Sketch of JK's character as it seemed to me. Probably written by Ellen Thun, dated 6/3/91: 1.

46. *Ibid*, 1.

47. *Ibid*, 1.

48. Ellen Thun, Heartwarmers: Current Topic Board; Assassination, Korea Times. November 26, 1996.

49. Bong-youn Choy, *Koreans in America* (Chicago: Nelson Hall Press, 1979), 92–94.

50. Wayne Patterson, *Korean Frontier in America* (Honolulu: University of Hawaii Press, 1988) 48–50. There was some scandal when several planters attempted to enforce repayment of the passage by imported laborers, however, Wayne Patterson argues that repayment became an individual responsibility rather than an obligation when contract-labor system became illegal.

51. Ellen Thun, "Heartwarmers" Korea Times. January 4, 1995: 3.

52. Easurk Emsen Charr, *The Golden Mountain: The Autobiography of a Korean Immigrant 1895–1960*, ed. Wayne Patterson, 2nd ed. (Urbana and Chicago: University of Illinois Press, 1996), 151. N. Kim's Korean name is In Soo Kim. According

to Ralph Ahn (youngest son of Ahn Chang Ho), In Soo Kim urged Dosan to come to Riverside to work and settle.

53. Ibid.

54. The Santa Fe rail station established in Riverside in 1890 became known as Pachappa Station, and Pachappa later lent its name to the avenue on which the camp and station stood. Following the construction of the railway, the housing proved no longer necessary for the intermittent Chinese workers who either moved to another settlement in the city or followed work elsewhere. Mary Paik Lee, *Quiet Odyssey: A Pioneer Korean Woman in America* (Seattle: University of Washington Press, 1990), 15.

55. Ellen Thun, Heartwarmers. Korea Times, January 4, 1995.

56. "Reviewing Our Past: Tracing Family Histories. Excerpt from November 1995 Video Shoot with Ellen Thun." Korean American Museum, December 1996.

57. Lee, *Quiet Odyssey,* 14.

58. Charr, 1961: 150–151.

59. Lee, *Quiet Odyssey;* Charr, *Golden Mountain.*

60. Ellen Thun, "Heartwarmers" Korea Times. October 29, 1996: 14.

61. Ibid.

62. Ellen Thun, "Heartwarmers" Korea Times. March 1, 1995: 3.

63. Ibid.

64. Lee, *Quiet Odyssey,* 14.

65. Ellen Thun, "Heartwarmers" Korea Times. October 29, 1996: 14.

66. Charr, *Golden Mountain,* 152.

67. Lee, *Quiet Odyssey,* 18.

68. *Press Enterprise,* March 6, 1921: 6.

69. Edward T. Chang and Woo Sung Han, *Korean Pioneer Aviators: The Willows Airmen* (Lexington Books, 2015), 55.

70. Lee, *Quiet Odyssey,* 17.

71. The Alien Land Law applied to aliens ineligible for citizenship, which included Koreans, Japanese, Indian, and Chinese immigrants.

*Quotes on pages 21 and 22 were misattributed in earlier printings of the book and have been corrected.

Chapter Two

Independence Movement and Korean National Association

PACHAPPA CAMP AS THE FOCAL POINT
OF THE INDEPENDENCE MOVEMENT

Pachappa Camp served a central role in assisting and organizing the larger Korean community. With Ahn Chang Ho as community leader and organizer, Koreans learned the true value of their work. Ahn did not consider any effort menial, but viewed his time spent cooking in the houses of Riverside's elites and picking fruit in orchards as opportunities to grow, study, and gain patience. Ahn told his coworkers in Riverside to pick with care to reduce spoilage, and he adopted techniques he learned from Rumsey, using a system developed by Harold Powell, to store oranges without harming the fruit.[1] Owners of local ranches thanked Korean workers for their care of the fruit: "You all work like the orange trees were yours—so carefully."[2]

Ahn led other workers to follow his example so that they, too, approached their work with care, diligence, and purpose, and earned the respect of Americans.[3] Thus, even the seemingly humble activities of daily life held great important for Dosan. Despite being underpaid and working undesirable jobs, the community saw the value of their work, the larger lessons they could gain from it, and allowed this understanding to foster a sense of community and purpose, which grew in scope with Japanese annexation of the Korean peninsula.

Ahn's ideas about education and meaningful work later stood as the basis for the Shanghai Korean Provisional Government in 1919, thus policies Ahn implemented in Riverside served larger purposes several years later.

The modest living conditions at Pachappa Camp both helped anchor the neighborhood's identity and reveal Koreans' struggle to support themselves and fight for Korean sovereignty. In 1905, the year Japan declared Korea a protectorate, Ahn and other community leaders, such as Yi Kang, established the *Gongnip Hyeophoe* (Cooperative Association) in Riverside.[4] They intended *Gongnip Hyophoe* to develop democratic policies and institutions among Koreans with the ultimate goal of founding a democratic Korean nation. By adhering to the Cooperative Association, residents of Dosan's Republic created complex social networks that helped tie them together, allowing for collective problem solving and promoting solidarity.

The *Gongnip Hyeophoe* created its own policing system in which agents could enter others' houses at will. It required residents to turn off their lights at nine at night, prohibited Korean women from smoking long pipes in the street, and enforced a dress code, forbidding anyone from going outside in an undershirt and encouraging the dawning of a white shirt when possible.[5] These rules hoped to instill positive virtues within its residents in addition to maintaining order. Likewise, the rules allowed greater cohesion to grow among the residents. All the community members agreed upon and followed the regulations, and the dress code demarcated residents of the settlement and followed Dosan's philosophy of raising Koreans to command respect in America because of their clean appearance. The Cooperative Association helped individuals to learn of work and educational opportunities. Having multiple branches of the *Gongnip Hyophoe* in Riverside; San Francisco; Redlands; and even Rock Springs, Wyoming; helped individuals to maintain contact, and to gain information about hospitable regions with ready work.[6]

Events in Korean American history would later coalesce the Cooperative Association's role in the independence movement and in uniting the Korean community. In 1908, two Koreans in San Francisco assassinated diplomat Durham White Stevens due to his anti-Korean policies and publicity campaign. At the time, Stevens served as foreign affairs advisor to Korea and as advisor to the Japanese Resident General, informing Japan of Korean internal affairs. The *San Francisco Chronicle* published remarks he made which claimed Koreans were unfit to govern themselves, illiterate and backward, and that Japan's control of Korea benefited the country and its people.[7] The Korean community in America, knowing of the subjugation of Koreans in the peninsula, were outraged by Stevens' remarks, and two individuals, Chang In-hwan and Chun Myung-woon, decided to take direct action.

The two patriots confronted Stevens at the San Francisco Ferry Terminal before he continued his anti-Korean publicity campaign. Chun Myung-woon assaulted Stevens while Chang In-hwan fired the fatal shots, while also wounding Chun. At the time, U.S. law prohibited Asians from owning firearms, so Chang's ability to procure a gun proved quite surprising.[8] At the time of the attack, Chang and Chun both belonged to Korean organizations in the United States. Chang was a member of the *Daedong Bogukhoe* (Great Eastern Protection Association), and Chun was a member of the *Gongnip Hyophoe*. In a show of solidarity, following Stevens' assassination, the *Hanin Hapsong Hyophoe* (United Korean Society), a conglomeration of Korean associations based in Hawaii, and the *Gongnip Hyophoe* merged on February 1, 1909, to form the Korean National Association (KNA). Merging mainland and Hawaiian associations into one organization to oversee the two patriots' defense and Korean interests abroad helped unite Koreans in America, allowing them to better organize and work for freedom. The Korean National Association filled much the same role as the *Gongnip Hyophoe*, but further promoted patriotic initiatives in an effort to free Korea of Japanese influence.[9] Although Dosan was in Korea and engaged in secret Shinminhoe activities, he was involved and still considered a strong leader and founder of the Korean National Association. On October 26, 1909, the news of the assassination of Prince Ito in China, reached Koreans living at Pachappa Camp. Ellen Thun vividly described the excitement and activity of Pachappa Camp at the time when it got the news of Ito's death at the hands of a Korean nationalist.

Pachappa camp was the center of activity again. Nightly meetings were held in the mission house and funds for Chung-kun Ahn's defense were collected. The Chuns attended and Mr. Chun said the cost of the horse and buggy was worth it. He pledged an amount which his wife would later take him to task for when they reached home. But her protest would be half-hearted; other wives would, like her, be giving their husbands an earful not really meaning it. For there was not a single Korean who could repay Patriot Ahn for his courageous deed. So it was an evening of speeches and promises. Men and women rose and told of heroic actions in former times, and prayed they were strong enough to carry on the burden of Korea's freedom. There was much haranguing of the enemy, with a long list of grievances because each speaker had suffered imprisonment, torture, or loss.[10]

The news of the assassination of Ito also inspired Koreans living at Pachappa Camp to practice firing guns in order to prepare to fight against Japanese imperialism. The Chun family obtained a firearm, and Ellen Thun's father, Mr. Chun, showed the gun to his children.

Mr. Chun opened the wrapping encasing. "A pistol!" his boys shouted. Mr. Chun lifted the gun carefully and said, "It is an Iver-Johnson, secondhand from the pawnshop." Mrs. Chun sat down heavily: she had not yet had her baby, which was due very soon. Her comment: "*Aigo.*" Mr. Chun explained, "Someday we will have to fight to regain our country. First we learn to shoot, like Chung-kun Ahn. Ready! Aim! Fire! That is how you begin."[11]

Mr. Chun's acquisition of a firearm and the story about Pachappa residents practicing for a fight against Japan confirms that Pachappa Camp was the center of the early Korean independence movement in the United States, and they were willing to not only take guns and rifles but also sacrifice themselves for the freedom of their homeland.

Residents at Pachappa held numerous independence activities including a mock funeral service designed to protest Japan's forced colonization of Korea. However, women were not allowed to participate directly at the meeting. Ellen Thun vividly described how this protest meeting was held; a gong sounded for the people to be seated; the women left."

> Mr. Song was calling the people to order. The Korean national anthem opened the meeting. Ai Kook Ka (Korean National Anthem) was to the tune of *Auld Lang Syne*. . . . We know what we must do: Fight on for Korea's freedom. There is no other choice. Our leaders will be returning, those who escaped the Japanese network, to Manchuria, China, Hawaii, Cuba, Mexico, Siberia, and our own Mr. Ahn. Note that these are Overseas Koreans now. It is the Overseas Koreans who are given the torch to carry on the fight for freedom. Mr. Ahn comes through Europe without papers. All passports issued under the king and Korean government have been cancelled by the Japanese. Koreans are now Japanese subjects and must carry Japanese documents. Mr. Ahn is Korean! He must travel a man without country, alone.' He paused, visibly struggling with his feelings. . . . The clapping never stopped because it went on and on in the hearts of the listeners who passed on the secret meaning: Forever Korean freedom! Fight! Koreans living at Pachappa Camp were undeterred and continued their fight to achieve independence of Korea.

With return of Dosan Ahn Chang Ho to Riverside, the Pachappa Camp became the center of the early Korean independence movement in the United States. Ahn returned to the United States as "a man without country" determined to fight for independence of Korea.

KOREAN NATIONAL ASSOCIATION OF
NORTH AMERICA DELEGATE CONVENTION (1911)

Dosan Ahn Chang Ho left for Korea in 1907 to fully engage in secret *Shinminho* (New People's Society) activities. Members of the New People's Society were arrested and imprisoned and Korea was colonized by Japan in 1910. Dosan decided to return to the United States to organize the Korean immigrant community in the U.S. and continue his independence activities. Dosan Ahn Chang Ho fled to China and finally returned to New York in September 1911 via Russia and Europe. Ahn Chang Ho stayed in New York for a week and left for San Francisco. Ahn travelled across the United States from New York, San Francisco, and Los Angeles, and finally arrived in Riverside where his wife and family members gladly welcomed him back.[12] In anticipation of Dosan Ahn Chang Ho's arrival to San Francisco, the *Sinhan Minbo* published, "Welcome Ahn Chang Ho," an article that ran on September 13, 1911. In addition, the *Sinhan Minbo* also published Dosan Ahn Chang Ho's speech on October 4, 1911.

> When I left Korea toward San Francisco, I felt pain and agony as I left them in Korea. My fellow comrades will face many serious problems and even torture in Korea, but I feel guilty as I escaped by myself. After I landed in New York and travelled across the United States, I was able to meet with fellow Koreans and felt glad to do so . . .[13]

Ahn Chang Ho praised how the Korean immigrant community developed during his five-year absence, but also urged them to prepare for an independence war. However, he was not referring to war against Japan with tanks or warships. "We must win against Japan in every aspect, including accumulation of capital, intellectual capabilities, study, labor, and trade." By this point in his life, Ahn Chang Ho believed that the independence of Korea by armed struggle was not possible and urged his fellow Koreans to study, accumulate wealth, and develop skills to achieve Korea's freedom.

Finally, Dosan Ahn Chang Ho returned to Riverside where his wife, Helen, and their children were anxiously awaiting. Ellen Thun described the Dosan Ahn Chang Ho's reunification with his family as follows:

> Did he rush home to Riverside where his wife and family awaited him? He hurried, yes, to take the train to San Francisco, and there stopped for association business. Then went on to Los Angeles, where his wife and son Philip met him because more association work had to be taken care of there. Mrs. Ahn had planned a surprise for his homecoming. When did she find the right moment to tell him? He had been in demand by everyone! She found time to tell him somehow. "I have three hundred dollars I earned while you were away, doing sewing and laundry and cooking for the workers." She held out the money. His face showed his amazement as he said, "This is a miracle!" and explained his remark. He recounted how Yi Kap, another independence fighter like himself, was with him coming to America when he was taken ill. After the friend was declared out of danger, he was severely handicapped and bedridden, and was without funds. The Korean National Association funds were low at the moment, and he said to his wife, "Would you consent to my sending Yi Kap the three hundred dollars? His need is greater than ours. And I will be going to work and earn money for us." Mrs. Ahn was an understanding wife. She knew this was her husband's way, and she said, "Yes." Her lady friends . . . because they were curious, quizzed her, "Has your husband changed very much since he has been

gone?" (They had heard where her three hundred dollars had been sent). She smiled and said, "No, he is the same Chang-Ho Ahn I love."[14]

Between 1909 to 1911, the Korean National Association of North America went through a stagnant period without their leader Ahn Chang Ho. When Ahn Chang Ho returned to Riverside in 1911, the Korean National Association found a renewed sense of independence activism. In 1911, Riverside hosted the Korean National Association of North America delegate's convention, revealing the importance of that branch and its devotion to the independence movement. At the convention one of the delegates, Kang Myeong-wha, remarked that the implementation of the Cooperative Association and its successor the KNA, formed the basis of a "splendid Dosan's Republic" in Riverside.[15]

It is important to note that the Korean National Association of North America Delegate Convention was held in Riverside in November 1911 right after Dosan Ahn Chang Ho returned from Korea. Why and what is the historical meaning of the KNA of North America Delegate Convention being held in Riverside? The *Sinhan Minbo* published an article on November 22, 1911, which offers some insight:

> Korean National Association of North America Delegate Convention will be held in Riverside on November 22 to review last year's activities and plan and decide the future of the organization. Delegates should participate with the deep sense of responsibility and decide on policy issues.

We can assume that Riverside was chosen as the site of the KNA of North America Delegate Convention because Dosan Ahn Chang Ho returned from Korea and his family was still residing in Riverside. At the time, Pachappa Camp was the largest and perhaps most active center of the independence movement in the United States. Dosan Ahn Chang Ho participated as the San Francisco delegate despite the fact that his family was living in Riverside. More importantly, all nine local chapter delegates attended the convention. They studied and discussed issues for ten days and passed twenty-one articles.[16] The *Sinhan Minbo* reported that the delegate convention began on November 23 at 2:00 p.m. and ended on December 4 at 2:30 a.m.[17]

Several important decisions were decided during the convention in Riverside: (1) The *Sinhan Minbo* was declared the "official bulletin" of the Central Council of the Korean National Association, and (2) The Korean National Association of North America headquarters would relocate from San Francisco to Los Angeles. But the Central Council of the Korean National Association headquarters would remain in San Francisco. By relocating the headquarters of the Korean National Association of North America to Los Angeles, it declared that the Central Council of the Korean National Association served as the supreme organ of all Koreans abroad, and (3) Previously, revenue of the Korean National Association was collected by monthly dues and contributions, but it was decided to combine the dues and collect a $5 annual duty fund. The Central Council of the Korean National Association allocated an annual budget, based on the mandatory annual $5 duty fund.[18] In addition, new endowment fund was created in order to establish the North American Industrial Company to accumulate capital. Ahn Chang Ho and In Soo Kim played key roles in establishing the North American Industrial Company. Lastly, the Korean National Association established its Education Bureau to teach future leaders of the Korean community. A *Sinhan Minbo* reporter who recorded notes, was thrilled with the new direction of the KNA; he "threw away his pen and got up [and] shouted Korean National Association, *Mansei Mansei Mansei*."[19] The Central Council of the Korean National Association declared itself as an "intangible government" of Korea. The Korean National Association proclaimed "Republicanism" and that it was governed by constitutional law.[20] For the first time, all nine local chapter presidents except Mexico (due to distance), attended the 1911 Korean National Association of North America delegate convention in Riverside. Ellen Thun, who was born in Riverside, vividly recalled how Ahn Chang Ho returned to Riverside and stirred the hearts and minds of the Korean youth. She recounts how, during Dosan's stay in Riverside, he urged her young cousins, Frank and Jacob, to fight for the independence of Korea:

> Mr. Ahn was returning to Riverside; he had been at it a long time. Over a year. ". . . They had power. And it was taken away. I wept there; yes I wept coming homeward. The weeping is over. We start work here, it is up to us, the overseas Koreans. We stand up for Korean independence!" The older man looked at the boys keenly. Then asked, "Is your mind-set nara-il?" Two heads nodded. He said, "You will continue to study to return to serve the people. And you will fight for independence!" He rose from his chair and went over to pick up a package he had left on a side table. He gave it to Frank who was the older brother. "This is entrusted to your safekeeping. Open." Frank opened the wrapping which revealed a silk scarf that held Mr. Ahn's gift. Frank put the present in front of Jacob and together they untied it. Folded there was the Korean flag. Mr. Ahn said. "I could not bring the country with me, into exile, and give it to you for safekeeping. I bring instead this symbol, Taeguk-ki. Restore it when you return to our homeland."[21]

During Dosan Ahn Chang Ho's absence, the Korean National Association of North America was floundering with lack of leadership and resources. However, with the return of Dosan Ahn Chang Ho, the Korean National Association of North America restructured its organization, established rules and regulations, and the future direction of independence movement in the United States. It confirms that Riverside's Pachappa Camp was the "home" of early Korean immigrants and functioned as the center of the Korean independence movement.

The *Sinhan Minbo* (November 22, 1911) reported that the Korean National Association of North America convention would be held at Riverside. But, why Riverside? Not only did Dosan and his family reside in Riverside, but more importantly, Pachappa Camp was the center of the Korean immigrant community and focal point of the independence movement in the United States at the time. The *Sinhan Minbo* (November 20, 1911) reported that the Riverside Korean community under the leadership of In Soo Kim (distant relative of Helen Ahn), was well prepared to welcome delegates of the KNA. In other words, Pachappa Camp was one of the most well-organized Korean immigrant communities at the time and was able to host the national convention. The Korean National Association of North America convention meeting began at 2:00 p.m. on November 23, 1911, and ended at 2:30 a.m. on December 4, 1911. "Nine chapter delegates attended the convention and discussed legislations for ten days and passed 21 resolutions. In particular, many delegates expressed their opinion and able to reach consensus."[22] During the convention, the Korean National Association of North America announced that its organization was a Republican system and would uphold constitutional law. "Elected representatives of the Korean National Association of North America have rights to legislate rules and regulations, appoint executive board, pass budget and others. Delegates will meet once a year to vote on budget and other related matters."[23] According to the *Sinhan Minbo*, the Korean National Association of North America convention held in Riverside in 1911 was the first and last time all local chapter presidents attended a KNA meeting. "Afterward, chapter presidents failed to attend convention[s] and instead authorized members residing in San Francisco to attend"[24] on their behalf.

Hyung-chan Kim misidentified a photo taken in 1911 as "the people in the photo gathered here at Tosan's place probably to commemorate the founding of the branch office of the Korean National Association." However, the Riverside chapter of the Korean National Association was the first local chapter of the organization and was established in 1909. The photo in question was actually taken in 1911, in Riverside, during the Korean National Association of North America convention. Also, during field research, I was able to locate another photograph of the residents of Riverside at Pachappa Camp during that same period. The photo was disovered in the Catherine Violet Kim estate and was taken near the canal where Pachappa Camp was located. The people in the photo are wearing similar clothing to the one that Hyung-chan Kim misidentified.

The fact that the Korean National Association of North America convention was held in Riverside at Pachappa Camp, right after Dosan Ahn Chang Ho returned from Korea to the United States, has several historical significance factors: (1) Pachappa Camp was the home of Dosan Ahn Chang Ho's family, (2) It had infrastructure to hold national convention, (3) Under Dosan Ahn Chang Ho's leadership, the Korean National Association of North America was able to restructure and reorganize and energize the Korean independence movement in the United States.

One of the most puzzling facts is that Dosan Ahn Chang Ho's biographer, the *Heungsadan*, or the Korean National Association, all failed to mention that the Korean National Association of North America convention was held in Riverside in November 1911. What is the historical meaning of the Korean National Association convention being held in Riverside? It is my conclusion that the convention, which was held in Riverside for ten days right after Dosan Ahn Chang Ho's return to America from Korea, is one of the most important meetings that was convened in early Korean American history for several reasons: (1) Riverside is the birthplace of the Korean National Association of North America convention, (2) for the first and only time, all Korean National Association local chapter presidents attended the meeting, (3) rules and regulations of the Korean National Association of North America were discussed and passed by delegates, and (4) Riverside's Pachappa Camp was the center of the early Korean independence movement in the United States. It was no accident that the Korean National Association of North America convention was held in Riverside on November 23, 1911. Not only did Dosan Ahn Chang Ho return from Korea and settled in Riverside, but also Pachappa Camp was the center of Korean immigrant settlement in the United States with infrastructure to hold national convention. Although the Korean National Association was established in 1909, the absence of its leader, Dosan Ahn Chang Ho, negatively impacted KNA activities. With the return of Dosan Ahn Chang Ho, the Korean National Association was able to restructure and reinvigorate organizational activities and increase in membership. Dosan Ahn Chang Ho's second stay in the United States, 1911–1919, was probably the most active period of his activities in America, and it all began with the 1911 KNA North America convention in Riverside.

THE GREAT FREEZE OF 1913 AND THE CLOSURE OF THE RIVERSIDE CHAPTER OF THE KNA

Known as the Great Freeze of 1913, the terrible freeze devastated the orange industry in Riverside. Many Korean citrus workers packed up and moved to central California and elsewhere after the crops failed. According to Joan Hall, "production decreased from 15,273,000 boxes in 1912 to less than half at 6,870,000 boxes in 1913. Numerous families lost their groves and even their homes when banks foreclosed on unpaid mortgages. Moving companies were kept busy throughout the citrus belt when families were uprooted and had to give up their dreams of becoming prosperous citrus growers."[25] Unable to secure employment, many Korean laborers began relocating to Central California cities including Reedley and Dinuba. Others moved to northern California cities like Willows or Sacramento. Dosan Ahn Chang Ho and his family also relocated to Los Angeles sometime between October and December 1913. Initially, I thought the "Great Freeze of 1913" shut down Pachappa Camp and the Korean community in Riverside. However, Pachappa Camp survived and existed until November 1918. According to a *Sinhan Minbo* December 12, 1918 article, the Riverside chapter of the Korean National Association relocated from 1532 Pachappa Avenue to nearby 1158 Vine Street.

While it is unclear exactly when Dosan moved to Los Angeles, a *Sinhan Minbo* report indicated that Ahn resided in Riverside as of September 1913.[26] However, a *Sinhan Minbo* report dated October 10, 1913, stated that Ahn was being treated for an illness at the 7th Adventist Hospital near Riverside and returned to his residence in Los Angeles. Therefore, it is clear that Ahn Chang Ho and his family were residing in Los Angeles as of October 1913. Pachappa Camp continued to function as the "home" and location of early Korean independence movement activities, despite the number of Korean residents declining after the 1913 Great Freeze.

According to a *Sinhan Minbo* report dated September 6, 1917, the "Riverside chapter of the KNA held a mournful ceremony of the 'National Humiliation Day' on August 29, and all 30 residents attended." As of August 1917, the number of Korean residents at Pachappa dwindled to thirty, and they faced economic hardships trying to maintain the Riverside chapter of the Korean National Association. "Riverside chapter decided to shut down for four months as many members are moving elsewhere." The Riverside chapter of the KNA tried to restructure and reorganize with the election of new officers on November 2, 1917: president, Jung Sup Koo; vice president, In Young Chung; general manager, Jae Duk Choi; secretary, Chang Man Kim; treasurer and educational affairs, Ryong Ju Kwak; judicial affairs; Il Woo Park, aid officer, Chul Ryang; and delegate, Soon Hak Kim.[27] However, the *Sinhan Minbo* reported on January 31, 1918, the news of the shutdown of the Riverside chapter of the KNA as follows:

Birthplace of the Korean National Association of North America is Riverside. Riverside chapter of the KNA is located at 1532 Pachappa Avenue for the past ten years. Riverside chapter of the KNA is beloved and respected by all members of the Korean National Association, but regrettable to hear recent news from Riverside chapter. "As of now, the total number of Riverside chapter resident is 45 including 15 men, 10 wives, and 20 children. However, only 4–5 individuals attend monthly meeting, only 15 attend church services, and unable to maintain Riverside chapter of the KNA. Therefore, we decided to close Riverside chapter building."

The *Sinhan Minbo* report clearly stated that Riverside is the birthplace of the Korean National Association of North America and that it regretted to hear the news of closure. Riverside KNA members must have debated fiercely on the future of the Riverside chapter. Two weeks later, the *Sinhan Minbo* (February 14, 1918) reported a rebuttal statement by the Riverside KNA members:

Riverside chapter members rebutted the *Sinhan Minbo* news of the closure of the Riverside chapter of the KNA building. We are unable to verify who spread the news of shut down of the Riverside chapter of the KNA, but we are disturbed by this news report. In recent years, many Korean citrus workers moved elsewhere due to bad harvest of oranges. Small number of Korean residents in Riverside have dedicated themselves for Korean National Association. We are very proud of the fact that we have been able to maintain Riverside chapter of the KNA with small members. We were able to pay off debt of the Riverside chapter of the KNA recently. Almost 20 people including men, women and children attend Korean language school every week. How can we close historic Riverside chapter of the Korean National Association?

On February 1, 1918, the Riverside chapter of the KNA held a ceremony to commemorate the founding of the Korean National Association. Despite financial difficulties and dwindling membership, the Riverside chapter of the KNA was hanging on and trying to maintain its KNA building. Ultimately, the Riverside chapter of the KNA was forced to shut down as it faced harsh financial difficulties. According to a *Sinhan Minbo* report dated April 19, 1918, "Since we are unable to maintain the Riverside chapter KNA building, we decided to combine church and Riverside chapter of the KNA. On November 10, 1919, Riverside chapter of the KNA moved from 1532 Pachappa Ave to 1158 Vine Street."[28] Thus, Pachappa Camp no longer functioned as a Koreatown. Only a small number of remaining Riverside Korean residents continued to maintain Korean ethnic identity, educate their children, and kept active in the independence movement.

THE HEMET VALLEY INCIDENT (1913)

The Riverside KNA played an integral role in achieving de facto diplomatic representation for the association of Koreans in America. During an event known as the Hemet Valley incident in 1913, an angry mob chased Korean fruit pickers from Riverside California, prompting the Korean and international communities to action. The apricot crop that year had been exceptionally plentiful, and ranchers feared a loss of profits if they could not secure sufficient labor to pick the fruit. The previous year, farmers had lost sizeable portions of their harvest because of a labor shortage.[29] Two ranchers in the Little Lake district of Hemet thus hired eleven Korean workers from Riverside through employment agent Choe Soon-sung at a lower wage than white workers.[30] When the pickers arrived in Hemet, their employer did not meet them at the train station, and they loitered in the area, awaiting further instruction. In the interim, a mob formed, unhappy about seeing Asian workers in their town. Under the impression that the Koreans were Japanese, the spokesman of the crowd stated they "told the Japanese that they were not wanted in Hemet or its vicinity, as it was intended to maintain Hemet Valley as a "white man's valley."[31]

Under fear of violence, the Koreans immediately fled the city on the next westbound train.[32] According to contradictory reports of this incident by various newspapers, it was unclear how many Korean workers were involved and where they came from.[33] While some press coverage of the incident claimed the workers came from Los Angeles, Korean language sources, such as the *Sinhan Minbo*, note the workers were hired through the Riverside employment agency labor contractor Choe Soon-sung and they were from Riverside.[34] A *Los Angeles Times* June 28, 1913, article also confirmed that Korean workers were from Riverside. These discrepancies in the press likely stem from the republication of misinformation caused by communication barriers between journalists and the persons involved.

Because the Hemet Valley incident occurred just after the ratification of the 1913 California alien land law, the issue quickly escalated into an international episode. At the same time the angry mob chased the Koreans out of Hemet, Japanese consuls were visiting San Francisco to battle the California legislature about the ratification of the law.[35] The Japanese government, with its strong ties to America, felt especially insulted that this law discriminated against its emigrants. When the Japanese Association of Southern California (JASC) learned of the Hemet incident, its secretary H. Wakabayashi contacted Riverside's Japanese Association for more information regarding the workers' expulsion. Wakabayashi learned the workers were in fact not

Japanese, but nonetheless claimed authority over the Koreans, viewing them as subjects of Japan, and he consequently promised to seek indemnification for the workers. The JASC notified the Japanese consulate in San Francisco, which in turn informed the Japanese embassy in Washington, DC. The embassy then announced it would carry out an investigation.[36]

Having already set up neighborhood organizations and the Korean National Association to promote Koreans' rights, leaders in the Korean community had networks in place to combat this infringement on their right to self-representation. Riverside's KNA played a crucial role in mitigating the situation by informing other association branches of the gravity of the situation, allowing the Korean community to take immediate diplomatic action. With their strong national sentiment, Koreans refused to accept Japanese hegemony in America, their adoptive homeland. Having previously served on the Riverside KNA board of trustees in 1911, Choe Soon-sung, the employment agent who contracted the pickers, worked to secure indemnification for the workers' train fares, so none of the men incurred any financial loses.[37] In San Francisco, David Lee, the president of the North America Conference of the KNA, implored U.S. officials to consider Koreans in America apart from the Japanese. Lee directed a telegram to the Secretary of State William Jennings Bryan affirming:

> We, the Koreans in America, are not Japanese subjects. . . . We will never submit to her as long as the sun remains in the heavens. The intervention of the Japanese Consulate-General in Korean matters is illegal, so I have the honor of requesting you to discontinue the discussion of this case with the Japanese government representatives. . . . We will settle it without Japanese interference.[38]

Lee asserted that the Koreans involved in the Hemet incident immigrated to the United States before Japan colonized Korea, and that Japan therefore had no claim in representing these Koreans' interests abroad. Attempting to represent these non-subjects amounted to an infringement upon the Koreans' rights. Hoping to settle the conflict without the added formalities of satisfying Japanese diplomats, Secretary of State Bryan responded positively to Lee's bequest, and on July 2, 1913, he announced a distinction to be made between Korean and Japanese in America.[39] A *San Francisco Call* July 2, 1913, article reported that, "Hemet Korean Incident closed by Bryan's Order." Secretary Bryan declared that fruit pickers expelled from the California town of Hemet were not subjects of Japan.

> Investigation by agents of the state department of the recent expulsion of a number of Korean fruit pickers from Hemet, was ordered discontinued today and the

incident is considered closed. Secretary Bryan, who had ordered the inquiry on his own initiative, particularly on account of the pending negotiations between the United States and Japan over the Californian alien land legislation, received a telegram from president of the David Lee Korean National association informing him that the Koreans involved were not Japanese subjects, because they had left their native land before it was annexed by Japan.

The significance of the Hemet Valley incident is that it allowed for the unofficial recognition of Koreans as not Japanese subjects. The unofficial recognition allowed for Koreans in America to do two things: (1) Korean immigrants in America could continue the independence movement in the U.S. and include direct armed resistance. The status and treatment of Koreans in America contrasted sharply with Asian Indians in the United States. Asian Indian Americans also started an independence movement against British colonialism in the United States. However, unlike Korean American organizations like the KNA, Asian Indian American independence groups were labeled as terrorists and many leaders were arrested, imprisoned, and deported. (2) Korean immigrants entering the U.S. could enjoy an easier entry process into the U.S. compared with Chinese and Japanese. Korean immigrants who landed in San Francisco without visas or student documentation often claimed that they were students, not laborers. With the sponsorship of the KNA, most Korean workers were allowed to enter the United States without too much hassle. The Hemet incident revealed the multiple challenges the Korean population faced in the United States. Due to the colonization of the peninsula and a lack of cultural education about Asians, many Americans often associated Koreans with the Japanese, causing further strife for Korean immigrants. In this case, U.S. citizens mistreated Koreans because of a perceived association and conflation of identities with the Japanese, demonstrating how Koreans in America experienced negative imperial influences at home and abroad. The Hemet incident, while revelatory of the racial tensions in southern California at the time, also proved an important moment for the KNA to maintain legitimacy in representing Koreans in America.

WOMEN WARRIORS

Unlike other Korean immigrant communities during the early twentieth century, Pachappa Camp was family-based with many women and children. Women played a central role at the camp, responsible for cooking, cleaning, child-rearing, and they were the gatekeepers of the community. And yet, history is often written by men from a male perspective, and the role of women are often minimized at best. In the beginning, women at Pachappa Camp mostly played secondary roles to the men. Women were mostly responsible for taking care of children, household chores and cooking for bachelors. Ellen Thun said that her mother was not actively involved in the Korean National Association and had too many children.

> No, she went to a few meetings when they first came to Riverside. But, one of the women later told me, she said "Oh, your poor mama, she only came to the meeting when she still had silk dresses from Korea. Then, there was no money for silk dresses; she never came to our meetings. Poor thing." But, she meant that my mother had too much pride. But, the thing was by that time all that was happening with the meeting, my mother had too many children and she had to stay home to take care of the children you know right after the other. And this was something I know that my cousin Jacob felt that my father was very wrong and having so many children because after I was born, the doctor was very concerned about my mother's mental health. So, he had my cousin come into town and explained about birth control and use condoms. And he gave a set to Jacob to take back to dad and explain. And he explained that our mother was mentally very fragile that it would just take a little bit more and she'll be knocked out. But, my father never took that seriously. And after I was born, there were 3 more children, one right after the other.[40]

Busy with child rearing, taking care of household chores, and working side-by-side with men, the women of Pachappa Camp provided stability and a sense of community. Interestingly, the women of Pachappa Camp must have enjoyed relatively free lifestyles compared with women in Korea. "Korean women in Riverside and Redlands are riding bicycles very well." The *Gongnip Sinbo* reported this interesting story on December 21, 1905. Not only is this an interesting story, but it is also groundbreaking news of Korean women riding bicycles at a time when Korean women were not even allowed to have face-to-face meetings with men in Korea. Korean women living at Pachappa Camp must have enjoyed relative degrees of freedom and openness compared with women in Korea. Women at Pachappa Camp not only were responsible for domestic chores and child rearing, but also worked side by side with the men. The early Korean immigrant community men outnumbered women considerably, and yet, these small number of Korean women worked, sacrificed, and served as the backbone of the early Korean immigrant community because they provided stability and familial cohesiveness, as well as income. The contributions of Korean women in forming family, community, and the early independence movement should be properly recognized.

Ban Suk Lee, wife of Ji Young Chung, served as a teacher for the Korean school at Pachappa Camp. According to a *Sinhan Minbo* article dated April 29,

1915, "Korean residents in Riverside hold bible studies every Sunday. Fifteen adults attend bible studies and elder Do Won Ha who recently came from Korea, serves as a teacher. ten children also attend bible studies and this class is taught by Ban Suk Lee, wife of Ji Young Chung." Ban Suk Lee not only served as a teacher for the Korean school, but also contributed to the well-being of her family psychologically and economically. The obituary of Ban Suk Lee by the *Sinhan Minbo* published on March 30, 1939, reads as follows: "She is from Pyongyang, and came to America in 1915. She married with Ji Young Chung, and raised 3 sons and 2 daughters for the past 29 years. She was responsible for children's education, helped economically, and sacrificed for public interest."

Jung Sung Cha was the wife of Jung Suk Cha and she lived in Riverside for five years, beginning in 1906. She passed away in San Francisco on March 26, 1944. Her obituary reads:

> She was 59 years old and came from Pyongyang, Korea. She married Jung Suk Cha in 1902 and joined her husband in Hawaii who arrived a year ago. They relocated to the mainland in 1906 and resided in Riverside for 5 years. They again moved to Pasadena and lived for 29 years. Two years ago [they] moved to San Francisco. She stayed with her husband, attended church, and contributed for [the] betterment of society . . .[41]

During the early period of the Korean independence movement, contributions by women to the movement were limited to donating to the duty fund. Many women contributed to the fund and they included: the mother of Chan Bong Song who contributed one dollar, Helen Ahn one dollar, Mrs. Cha one dollar, and Bo Pae Lim one dollar.[42] Mrs. Cha is Jung Suk Cha's wife, Helen Ahn is wife of Ahn Chang Ho, and Bo Pae Lim is the eldest daughter of Jun Ki Lim. The *Sinhan Minbo* also reported that Chi Sam Song who resides in Riverside contributed $5 to support the *Sinhan Minbo*.[43]

Women who lived in Riverside appeared to have maintained close relationships and supported each other when needed. When the wife of Chi Sup Park heard Kyung Eui Lee was hospitalized, she sent relief funds. Although Park's family moved to Utah while ago, she sent money to help Kyung Eui Lee who was still residing in Riverside.[44] Interestingly, the wife of Chi Sup Park was white and she married Park several years prior to her friend's illness. Regardless of race, the women of Riverside appeared to have maintained very close relationships.

The independence of Korea had been declared in the streets of Seoul on March 1, 1919, with the people shouting "Mansei! Mansei!" Thousands and thousands of people came out on the streets and shouted, "Long Live Korea!" Pachappa Camp Koreans and students celebrated when they heard the news of the March 1 Mansei movement.

Mr. Choy began to sing the National Anthem of Korea and again the children followed in one voice. Now, he said as they finished. 'We will emulate the students in the homeland. We will demonstrate just like them!' He led them outside and told them to march to the corner and back. Willie Lee, the tallest, was flagbearer with Mr. Chun's two oldest sons as honor guards. Sam Kim who was the oldest stood by the teacher's side and saluted the flag and marchers. The marchers were five girls and three small boys. The day was not yet over. March First had only begun.[45]

Indeed, Pachappa Camp was a thriving Korean immigrant community and they were willing to sacrifice themselves for the independence of Korea. Pachappa Camp Koreans also played a critical role in establishing separate a "Korean identity" in America and rejecting the "Japanese subjects" label.

Although Pachappa Camp and the Riverside chapter of the Korean National Association of North America faced financial difficulties and declining membership as of 1918, Korean women became actively involved in the independence movement as they were allowed to become full members of the Korean National Association in January 1918. David Lee, president of the Korean National Association of North America, issued a proclamation on January 21, 1918: the "Korean National Association will allow women to become full members with rights and responsibilities equal to men."[46] Interestingly, the first women members of the Korean National Association of North America were Mexican women who married Korean men in Merida, Mexico.[47] In Riverside, Pachappa Camp women actively participated in ceremonies and independence related activities after 1918. On April 15, 1918, the Riverside chapter of the Korean National Association held ceremony to celebrate the establishment of Korean Provisional Government in Shanghai, China. A *Sinhan Minbo* article dated April 22, 1918, reported that the Korean national anthem was sung by Jung Sup Koo's wife, and a speech was delivered by the wife of Choong Sup Park, and prayers were said by the mother of Woon Kyung Lee.

The women of Pachappa Camp no longer played indirect roles, but now delivered main speeches during ceremonies and independence movement functions. In addition, the women of Riverside decided to take more direct actions and led a boycott of Japanese products. The *Sinhan Minbo* reported on the activities of the Korean women at Pachappa and published the following:

On September 16, 1918, women members of Pachappa camp decided to take full responsibilities to society as men. Mother of Woon Kyung Lee who is 60 years old was working hard at local hospital and she decided to contribute fund for national independence and society. Women of Pachappa camp also decided to make their own soy sauce at home and boycott Japanese products.[48]

Despite the KNA president's 1918 declaration that women could become full members of the association, the Riverside chapter didn't make their announcement official until a year later in 1919.[49] Thus, it should be recorded that women members of the Korean National Association of North America in Riverside played active roles as full members for independence of Korea at least since 1918, despite the its late announcement of the status of women as members.

In summary, the year 1918 was a pivotal moment for the women of Pachappa Camp. The number of Korean families significantly declined as many moved elsewhere in search of new employment opportunities. The Riverside chapter of the KNA relocated from Pachappa to nearby Vine Street. And yet, the women of Pachappa camp became more directly involved in the Korean National Association and independence movements despite the decline and relocation. There are three reasons why the women of Pachappa Camp became more active in the independence movement. First, in 1918, the Korean National Association changed by law to allow women as official members of the KNA.[50] Second, as the Korean population at Pachappa Camp declined, the role of women increased and they became an essential part of independence activities. Third, the March 1 Mansei movement ignited a new spirit of independence activism in both men and women.

NOTES

1. Vince Moses, "Oranges and Independence: Cornelius Earle Rumsey and Ahn Chang Ho; An Early East-West Alliance in Riverside, 1904–1911," *Riverside Museum Associates News Letter,* June 2000.

2. Ellen Thun, "Heartwarmers" Korea Times. February 1, 1995: 3.

3. Vincent Moses, "The Orange Grower is not a Farmer: G. Harold Powell, Riverside Orchardists, and the Coming of Industrial Agriculture, 1893–1930," *California History* 74 (1995): 22–37.

4. The Cooperative Association also known as the Mutual Assistance Association grew from Ahn's Friendship Society (Chinmok Hoe), Ahn's first overseas organization, which he established in San Francisco in 1903. After establishing the Cooperative Association, Ahn travelled to other Korean settlements in California, including Redlands and San Francisco to establish Kongnip Hyeophoe branches and observe the implementation of the association. Vince Moses, "Dosan Ahn Chang Ho: An American Pioneer," 2000; Sunju Lee, "Dosan Ahn Chang Ho's Activities in Riverside: 1904–1914," in *The Independence Movement and its Outgrowth by Korean Americans* (Los Angeles: Centennial Committee of Korean Immigration to the U.S., 2003), 111–192; Kim, *Tosan Ahn Ch'ang Ho.*

5. Kim, *Tosan Ahn Ch'ang Ho,* 35.

6. Wayne Patterson and Hyung Chan Kim, *The Koreans in America, 1882–1974: A Chronology & Fact Book* (Dobbs Ferry, NY, Oceana Publications, 1974).

7. *San Francisco Chronicle*, March 22, 1908.

8. The attack was covered extensively by the press; see "Adviser to Korea Shot by Oriental: D. W. Stevens Wounded in San Francisco." *Los Angeles Herald*, March 24, 1908; Stevens is Prominent in Diplomatic Circles." *Los Angeles Herald*, March 24, 1908.

9. Kim, *Tosan Ahn Ch'ang Ho,* 34.

10. Ellen Thun, Heartwarmers: Current Topic Board; Assassination, November 26, 1996.

11. *Ibid.*

12. *Sinhan Minbo*, September 13, 1911.

13. *Sinhan Minbo*, October 4, 1911.

14. Ellen Thun, "Heartwarmers: Afterward; Changes." *Korea Times*, February 25, 1997: 18.

15. Vince Moses, "Oranges and Independence: Cornelius Earle Rumsey and Ahn Chang Ho; An Early East-West Alliance in Riverside, 1904–1911," *Riverside Museum Associates News Letter,* June 2000.

16. *Sinhan Minbo*, December 11, 1911. Myung Wha Kang (President), Bun Kang (Chicago delegate), Jong Hyuk Kim (Claremont delegate), In Soo Kim (Riverside delegate), Chi Wan Lee (Redland delegate), Byung Ik Lee (Sacramento delegate), Jae Hyung Park (Los Angeles delegate), Chang Ho Ahn (San Francisco delegate), Sung Hwan Cho (Los Angeles delegate), Jung Suk Cha (Riverside delegate).

17. *Ibid.*

18. *Sinhan Minbo*, December 11, 1911.

19. *Ibid.*

20. *Sinhan Minbo*, December 5, 1911.

21. Ellen Thun, "Heartwarmers: Afterward: Changes" *Korea Times*, February 25, 1997: 18.

22. *Ibid.*

23. *Sinhan Minbo*, December 5, 1911.

24. *Sinhan Minbo*, December 20, 1917.

25. Joan H. Hall, A Citrus Legacy. Riverside, California: Highgrove Press, 1992: 119.

26. *Sinhan Minbo*, September 23, 1913.

27. *Sinhan Minbo*, November 29, 1917.

28. *Sinhan Minbo*, December 12, 1918.

29. "Little Brown Men are Not Welcomed." *Riverside Daily Press,* June 26, 1913, p. 3; "Hemet Expels the Yellow Men" *Los Angeles Times,* June 27, 1913; "All Quiet at Storm Center," *Riverside Daily Press,* June 28, 1913, p. 4.

30. *Sinhan Minbo*, July 4, 1913. However, Hyung-chan Kim and other newspaper report identified Korean workers were from Redland or Los Angeles.

31. "All Quiet at Storm Center," *Riverside Daily Press,* June 28, 1913, p. 4.

32. *Ibid.* Some secondary sources claimed the Koreans arrived at midnight (Moon, Kim), but they certainly arrived during the day when many individuals were about town. "Drive Asiatics from Town: Californians Thought Them Japanese, but Found Them Koreans." New York Times, 27 June 1913: 9. "All Quiet at Storm Center" *Riverside Daily Press,* June 28, 1913, p. 4.

33. Contradictory Information: *San Jacinto Register,* June 26, 1913: "15 Japs"; *Riverside (Enterprise?),* June 26, 1913: "About twenty Japanese and Koreans" From Riverside; *Riverside Enterprise,* June 30, 1913: "The spokesman then said, 'All right get our tickets and we will return to Los Angeles.'"; *Hemet News,* June 27, 1913: "train from Riverside brought about twenty Korean laborers"; *Hemet News,* July 4, 1913: "11 Korean fruit pickers": *Hemet News,* July 11, 1913: "Korean laborers comes from Los Angeles" according to Korean spokesperson; *Los Angeles Times,* June 27, 1913: "The noon train from Los Angeles brought twenty-five or thirty Japanese and Koreans, who had been employed by one of the Koreans to handle the apricot crop of the local rancher."; *Los Angeles Times,* June 28, 1913: "a party of Korean apricot pickers from Riverside"; *Riverside Enterprise,* June 30, 1913: "they were not wanted and should return to Los Angeles"; *San Francisco Call,* June 27, 1913: "15 Korean fruit pickers," "apricot picking crew of Koreans from Riverside"; *San Francisco Call,* 28 June 1913: "Korean apricot pickers from Riverside."

34. *Sinhan Minbo,* July 4, 1913.

35. "Dr. Soyeda Sure That in the End Californian Situation Will Be Settled Amicably," *New York Times,* June 26, 1913; "Tells Japan's Side Of California Case. State's Attitude Inconsistent with Our Previous Acts of Friendship, New Consul Says," *New York Times,* June 30, 1913.

36. Sucheng Chan, "Introduction" in *Quiet Odyssey,* xlix. "Little Brown Men are Ordered Back" June 27, 1913, *San Francisco Chronicle,* 3. "Expulsion Koreans Creates an International Situation," *Riverside Daily Press,* June 27, 1913, p. 6, the same article noted Japanese ambassador Sutemi Chinda would also likely order an investigation into the incident. *New York Times,* June 29, 1913: C4.

37. *Sinhan Minbo,* July 4, 1913.

38. Quiet Odyssey, L. originally quoted in *Sinhan Minbo* July 4, 1919.

39. *Los Angeles Times,* July 2, 1913, p. 14; *Hemet News,* July 4, 1913, p. 1; "Hemet Incident Considered Closed" *Riverside Daily Press,* July 2, 1913, p. 2.

40. Interview with Ellen Thun by Edward T. Chang on February 23, 1993, at her apartment in Los Angeles.

41. *Sinhan Minbo,* March 30, 1944.

42. *Sinhan Minbo,* June 30, 1909.

43. *Sinhan Minbo,* November 24, 1909.

44. *Sinhan Minbo,* March 14, 1918.

45. Ellen Thun, "Heartwarmers" Korea Times. March 1, 1995: 3.

46. *Sinhan Minbo,* January 24, 1918.

47. *Sinhan Minbo,* February 21, 1918.

48. *Sinhan Minbo,* September 18, 1918.

49. *Sinhan Minbo,* February 6, 1919.

50. *Sinhan Minbo,* January 24, 1918.

Chapter Three

Korean Mission and *Hakyo*

After long working days, members of the Korean community gathered at 1532 Pachappa Avenue, where residents established a community center. The center served many roles, among them a place of religious congregation. In 1906, residents established a mission at the site, under the care of the Calvary Presbyterian Church in Riverside.[1] By 1907, there were between fifty to sixty members who attended church services, held weddings, and baptized their children there. The *Riverside Enterprise* noted:

> The Korean mission . . . has only been established a year, but is a strong organization. A majority of the members are converts from the mission in Korea. There are between fifty and sixty members. Boys from the mission attend the Calvary church regularly. Young people from the mother church spend almost every evening teaching the young Koreans how to read and speak the English language.[2]

Noting the particularity of Riverside's community because of the number of families, the *Annual Report of the Board of Home Missions of the Presbyterian Church* described the Korean mission in Riverside as:

> Another happy group of Christians—somewhat distinguished from the other stations by the number of young wives and their children. They worship in a rented building, aided to some extent in the payment of the rent by the Calvary Presbyterian Church of Riverside. It is one of the most attractive spots in the far-famed-for-beauty town of Riverside.[3]

The Calvary Presbyterian Church of Riverside not only established a Korean Mission at Pachappa, but it also operated a night school to teach English to Korean immigrants. Easurk Emsen Charr recalled in his memoir:

On the very first evening of my arrival at the Korean camp, I met some of the night school teachers from the Presbyterian Church who were teaching my people English in the assembly room of the main red building, 1532 Pachappa Avenue, I remember, where they held Sunday services. I can still remember some of the teachers' names—a Miss White, a beautiful blonde young lady; Mr. and Mrs. Irvine; and Miss Patterson who was principal of the Irving School. And how kindly was the Rev. Alexander Aiken, who gave us immeasurable assistance and advise.[4]

The mission also hosted rites of passage for community members. Actor and eldest son of Ahn Chang Ho, Philip Ahn, was baptized in the mission. In addition to its role as a mission, the building served as a schoolroom as well, where first generation immigrants learned English in the evenings and, as time went on, where their children took Korean language classes. The building also held wedding receptions, and many couples such as Choong Sup Park and Dung Kyung Lee, who wedded in August 1915, married at the mission.[5] According to an invitation by Soon Hak Kim, a wedding reception for the new married couple was to be held at 1532 Pachappa Ave on August 7, 1915 at 7:30.[6] Mr. Soon Hak Kim (1876–1919) worked as a baker at the Glenwood Hotel (Mission Inn). He was also the Korean Mission pastor at Pachappa Camp in 1914. He passed away five years later in 1919, and he was buried at Evergreen Cemetery in Riverside. According to the *Sinhan Minbo* (March 6, 1919), "Soon Hak Kim Funeral Services. Forty-six Koreans and non-Koreans attended. Soon Hak Kim's funeral service were held at the Wimamstez (Korean translation unclear) Church on February 25 at 10:00 a.m. Nineteen individuals from Los Angeles, Upland, Claremont, fourteen non-Koreans, and thirteen people from Riverside; a total of forty-six people attended the funeral service. Reverend Chan Ho Min presided over the funeral service. People sang gospels and said prayers. Afterward, he was buried at the Evergreen Cemetery. Mr. Miller, one of Soon Hak's closest friends, invited all the guests to the Glenwood Hotel and served everyone lunch." Mr. Frank Miller was the owner of the Glenwood Hotel. At the time, it was highly unusual for a man like Mr. Miller to invite all the funeral guests for lunch at the hotel in honor of one of his Asian employees. It shows how much Mr. Miller respected Soon Hak Kim's character and his attitude toward racial minorities. On his headstone, the inscription says that Soon Hak Kim was a member of both the Korean National Association and the Young Korean Academy. He came to Hawaii with his wife on October 5, 1904, on the *S.S. Doric*. It is unclear exactly when he came to Riverside.

It appears that Reverend Samuel Moffett, who served as a missionary in Pyongyang, Korea, directly or indirectly helped to establish contact between the Riverside Calvary Presbyterian Church and the Pachappa Camp community members. According to a letter sent by Samuel A. Moffett to Dr. Brown,

> There are now in Riverside California some 30 or more Christians, already in touch with the Presbyterian pastor there and they are looking to our church to care for them. There are groups of Koreans in some 10 or 15 places where we have Christians and where I have no doubt we can organize little groups on the same plan as our work in Korea is organized, placing them in sympathetic, helpful touch with the Presbyterian churches in these places, holding their membership there and meeting with them if so desired but also holding separate services in Korean.[7]

Reverend Moffett wrote to Dr. Brown that "Mr. Pang visited Los Angeles, Riverside, Redlands and Pasadena and some other places."[8] Mr. Pang is Pang Hwa Joong, a son of Reverend Pang Ki Chang who became a minister in 1907. Reverend Pang Ki Chang is notable because he was one of the first seven Korean Presbyterian ministers in Korean history. Easurk Charr also described his encounter with Reverend Moffett in Pyongyang.

> Three of them were new to me—one woman and two men. The lady was Mrs. Lee, I think. One of the two men was blond-haired and bespectacled Dr. Wells, and the other was Ma Moksa (Rev. Samuel Moffitt) a slim, tall, handsome and young-looking man with light brown hair and mustache, blue eyes and a dimple at the point of his chin, and all smiles on his well-shaped and pink-cheeked face when he talked. And how well he could talk Korean![9]

According to Kang Yi, Ahn Chang Ho was asked to serve as missionary by white missionary in Pyongyang. However, he refused the offer because the church and white missionaries only emphasized evangelism and revivalism and disregarded oppression and colonial domination by the Japanese government. Dosan believed that Christians should be able to actively be involved in the fight for Korea's national independence while remaining religious. He firmly held that he could be a good Christian without the financial support of the church and still be politically active. Therefore, American missionaries in Korea disliked Dosan Ahn Chang Ho who was critical of conservative and evangelical Christianity in Korea at the time. In fact, the *Gongnip Sinbo* ran a critical article on May 20, 1908, about the Reverend Moffett who preached to only "believe in Jesus Christ" and disregarded social and political oppression. The article urged Koreans to participate for the independence of Korea. The *Sinhan Minbo* was also critical of the wife of Reverend Moffett who exploited a Korean lady by only paying $4 a month and treating her like her slave.[10] Dosan Ahn Chang

Ho and the Korean National Association viewed Christianity as a tool to achieve independence of Korea and opposed evangelism.

The links between Reverend Samuel Moffett in Pyongyang and the Riverside Korean Mission are now clearly established. Many Korean congregation members in Pyongyang must have had hopes similar to Charr's. "I wished that I could go to Me-Gook (America) someday and come back as a missionary to my native country!"[11] The closeness of the members of the church and the Pachappa residents can also be seen through a letter from Mrs. David Swims to Mrs. Helen Ahn. The letter shows Mrs. Swims' affection and love toward Mrs. Ahn and the Korean Mission at Riverside.

My dear Friend Mrs Ahn. Mr Ahn told me that Philson had been quite sickly but was better. I expect his [teeth] will be making trouble from now on and you will need to be very careful and not feed him anything. He is big and fat and that shows your milk is enough for him and as long as your milk is good do not feed him any thing else. I did not feed Cecilia any other food until she was 11 months old. I began to feed [J]ames at five months old and upset his stomach and he had bowel trouble for a long time I hope you keep well yourself and my big boy Philip tell him I hope he is a good boy and learning fast. Were you able to keep warm during the cold weather it was very cold here and I was sick in bed for nearly a week and then Cecilia was in bed for a few days. I hope Mrs. Y. K. Kim and Mrs Lim are well give them my love. I saw a notice in the papers telling of the death of Sarah Lee aged four years was that any of the Koreans—please tell me and tell me how everything at the Mission is. I think of you all everyday and pray for you. I go to the Mission here and enjoy seeing the faces I know and rejoice in their well doing. Peter Kim gave his lecture in the Central Church this week, but I did not see any Koreans present. I hope all can in Riverside will go to hear the lecture this week in the Y.M.C.A. Do you ever see Mrs. Evans or Mrs. Luogood? I hope they are well. Now my dear friend write me how is Robert he never writes me please tell him I think of him always and hope he is well and doing well. He can write in Korean to Mr Irvin will read it to me. Wish love to you and Mr Ahn and all the dear friends. I remain your friend. Mrs David Swims.[12]

The *Sinhan Minbo* also reported how there was a strong bond between Mrs. Stewart and Korean immigrants. "From Upland, Mrs. Stewart is a devoted Christian and special friend of the Korean people. Despite rising anti-Asian sentiment, Mrs. Stewart maintains friendship with many Koreans and welcomes them in her neighborhood."[13]

Church was not only place of worship but also a venue to discuss the political conditions of Korea. When Dr. Whiting, who had worked as a missionary in Korea, visited Riverside to give a talk, Mrs. Perry and Mrs. Stewart attended the special lecture in 1920. The *Sinhan Minbo reported on the event.*

On July 4, 1920, Dr. Whiting, who returned from Korea last September, came to Riverside Calvary Presbyterian Church to deliver a talk on the political situation of Korea to an American audience. In addition, he gave a talk in Korean at the Korean mission in Riverside. Korea has a long and rich cultural heritage and Koreans are peace loving people. Koreans are demanding freedom peacefully, and yet Japan brutally suppressed the Korean people with violence. Japan worships Nazism and what Japan has done to Korean people is like what the Nazis have done to the people of Belgium.[14]

After the lecture, Dr. Whiting went to Upland with Mrs. Stewart to give another talk. Catherine Violet Kim, youngest daughter of Yong Nun Kim, who was born and raised in Riverside, kept an old bible and hymn book, which was presumably used during the early twentieth century in Riverside and possibly at Pachappa Camp. The hymn book was printed in 1916 in Japan and published by American missionary Reverend Alexander Albert Pieters. He is the first American missionary to translate the Old Testament into the Korean language.[15]

Amazingly, Riverside Calvary Presbyterian Church kept old records and amazingly, among them were Korean membership lists, meeting notes, bulletins, and sessions of minutes. The records are contained in several bound books that survived the ravages of time. According to one record which shows the church's Korean membership list, Sun Kygrui Park, Chung Sam Kim and Chin Kuk Oh registered at Riverside Calvary church on June 29, 1905.[16] It notes that they came to Riverside in 1904 and many more Koreans were expected to attend church at their next meeting. Therefore, we know for sure that Korean immigrants began to settle in Riverside in 1904 or earlier. Chai Kwan Chung registered as church member on July 2, 1905. Church elder Cornelius E. Rumsey, who supported Dosan Ahn Chang Ho in establishing the Korean Labor Bureau in 1905, directly or indirectly helped to connect Korean immigrants to Riverside Calvary Presbyterian church.

Mr. and Mrs. Rumsey relocated to Riverside from Pittsburg on January 4, 1903, and registered at the Riverside Calvary Presbyterian church. Mr. Rumsey became church choir director on April 11, 1904, and began working at the Spanish mission on April 11, 1905. He later was appointed as president of the Spanish mission on July 23, 1905. In addition, he attended the church's elder meeting to discuss the Korean mission as well. Therefore, it is reasonable to assume that Mr. Rumsey must have played a role in connecting Korean immigrants with Riverside Calvary Presbyterian church.

A Riverside Calvary Presbyterian church Bulletin dated October 24, 1909, clearly shows both the Korean mission and Spanish mission on its front cover. The address of the Korean mission was 1532 Pachappa Avenue and the Spanish mission was located at 230 Eighth Street. When Riverside Calvary

Presbyterian church celebrated its 25th anniversary in 1914, S. H. Kim was in charge of the Korean mission. S. H. Kim is Soon Hak Kim, who was president of the Korean National Association of North America Riverside chapter and member of the Young Korean Academy. Tragically, he was killed in buggy accident in 1919 while working as a baker at the Glenwood Mission Inn; he was forty-three years old.

Based on the information gathered from the Calvary Presbyterian Church records, it appears that the Korean mission in Riverside did not have a full-time pastor. According to the *Sinhan Minbo*, Young Woon Moon was in charge of the Korean mission until early 1915, and Do Won Ha, who was an elder in Korea, took over and Jae Duk Cho was decon.[17] Reverend Chan Ho Min and Reverend Rokglin came to Riverside and preached the gospel.[18]

Riverside is place of good fortune and church has prospered in recent years. On March 30, Reverend Rokglin and Reverend Chan Ho Min came to Riverside to preach the gospel and many people attended services and refreshment afterward. Interestingly, Reverend Rokglin sang God's praises in Chinese and Mary Song sung in English. It appears that the Korean mission was prospering and very active during this time. In addition, the Korean mission held bible studies with fifteen adults who were led by Don Won Ha. The wife of Ji Young Chung, Ban Suk Lee, taught ten children at the Camp, thus demonstrating the Korean community's continued existence in 1915.[19]

Women of the Korean mission and Calvary Presbyterian church especially seemed to maintain very close relationships. The Women's Missionary Society at Calvary Presbyterian Church provided support services for the Korean women. On the afternoon of April 6, 1918, a friendship meeting was held at the Korean mission to promote ties between Korean women and American women. Approximately twenty Koreans and twenty Americans attended this meeting. Mrs. Man, Mrs. Pierson, and Mrs. Stevens were guests of honor. Although Mrs. Man was a poor old lady, she taught the English language to young Koreans and supported the Korean mission with all of her effort. The Korean mission expressed its heartfelt gratitude to Mrs. Man.[20]

As time went on, the residents of Pachappa Camp dwindled, and by 1918, a Riverside Calvary Presbyterian church bulletin dated November 17, 1918, no longer listed the Korean mission or the Spanish mission on its front page. It is unclear from the bulletin or the records if the Korean mission was no longer officially part of the Riverside Calvary Presbyterian church or if it became a separate, independent mission as of 1918. The Korean mission, whether part of the church or not, continued to exist and was combined with the Korean language school (*hakyo*). The Korean National Association of North America Riverside chapter relocated to nearby Vine Street in 1918, and that's where the mission and the *hakyo* combined space into one building. A photo taken in 1919 at Vine Street shows that Korean mission services were held two times on Sunday at 2:30 and Thursday at 8 p.m.

Much of the information about the Korean mission and the church members were found in the session of minutes and documents archive located at the Calvary Presbyterian Church in Riverside, CA. The session of minutes are detailed, handwritten records of church activities, members, and the admission of minority groups as part of the flock of worshipers. Korean members of the church were listed by name, year of admission, and even by departure date. For example, on December 2, 1914, it was recorded in a session of minutes that:

> The moderator reported that he and Elder Bayley had attending a meeting at the Korean Mission at which Dr. Laughlin, Fried Sea of the Foreign Mission Board for Koreans and Chinese was present. On examination of candidates on profession on faith was held and a Communion Service followed. Dr Hunger reported that the three Koreans named, Hak H. Lee, Jung S. Koo, Jung K. Kai, had made a good profession and he recommended that they be received into membership of the church. It was move seconded and adopted that they be so received.

The records found at Calvary Presbyterian Church provided insight and new information about the Korean American community known as Pachappa Camp in Riverside. Church bulletins and even the Women's Society's session of minutes provided insight into the lives of the Koreans at Pachappa. The Korean membership list of the church is included in the church register 1887–1899 records and noted as the Korean membership. In an added section after page 134 of the record—the pages were literally pasted into the book—a detailed list of each of the Koreans who joined the church is listed. The list continues to page 135. A total of fifty-three names appear. Koreans were already living in Riverside before joining the church and many submitted their formal petition to attend in 1905. Thus, the first recorded name on the Korean membership list in the record is dated June 29, 1905.

HAKYO: KOREAN SCHOOL

Korean immigrants at Pachappa Camp tried to learn English at the church night school while they taught Korean language and culture at the Korean School or *Hakyo* to their children. Easurk Charr recalled his first encounter with English night school: "On the very first evening of my arrival at the Korean camp, I met some of the night school teachers from the Presbyterian Church who were teaching my people English in the assembly room of the main red building, 1532 Pachappa Avenue, I remember, where they held Sunday services."[21] *Hakyo* was established as soon as Korean immigrants began to settle at Pachappa Avenue in Riverside in 1905. The *Gongnip Sinbo* reported night school activities in Riverside as follows: "President of *Gongnip Hyohoe*, Sung Moo Kim, also serves as the principal of night school in Riverside. Between 6–7 p.m. he teaches math to students. American women teacher teaches English between 7:30 and 9:00 p.m. to approximately seventeen to eighteen students."[22] It appears that Korean students and English teachers maintained good relations as reported by the *Gongnip Sinbo* on May 31, 1907. "Korean students at night school invited two women English teachers and had great time together." Easurk Charr also started to learn English at night school and he thought he was doing very well until he encountered a local shoe store clerk. "So, one day I went to a down town shoe store to buy me a new pair of Sunday shoes. This was the first pair of shoes I ever bought for myself. When the clerk asked me what size shoes I wore, I said, 'Half past five, mister.' Smiling, the clerk said, 'You mean you wear the size five and a half, don't you? We say 'half past five' when we speak of time only, you see.' Thank you, mister, I said."[23]

Children attended public schools and spoke English. They learned about America. Ellen Thun wrote about the contradictory feelings Korean immigrant parents felt about the Americanization of their children. "Uncle remarked, 'they are learning the American way fast.' Auntie voiced doubt which she had not been able to express before. They are forgetting they are Korean. Is that right for them? Is it good?"[24] The *Gongnip Sinbo* reported that Oak Ryong Kye, a member of the *Gongnip Hyophoe*, provided financial support to Chang Ryul Kim who came to America alone to study. Kim studied in Riverside and his parents, who resided in Korea, expressed gratitude to Mr. Kye.[25] Dung Lup Chung transferred from San Bernardino to Riverside school in 1906 and he registered at the Korean mission on April 28, 1907.[26] The *Gongnip Sinbo* reported four Korean students were attending school in Riverside and all of them were male students. "According to Chin Kuk Oh, Dung Lup Chung entered seventh grade, Kwan Yu Kim sixth grade, and Young Il Kim and Eui Suk Charr fourth grade when school opened in October this year." However, Young Il Kim entered sixth grade, not fourth grade as previously reported.[27] It appears that only a handful of Korean students attended regular public school as full time students during daytime. The majority of students worked during daytime and attended night school at Pachappa Camp. According to the *Gongnip Sinbo*, only six students attended regular public schools, and eighteen students studied at night school.[28] Chin Kuk Oh, who was in charge of the education of children at Pachappa Camp, played a major role in organizing and supporting the children's education. To ensure education of children, "Chin Kuk Oh donated $25 to support five Korean students who faced financial difficulties."[29]

Chungsurk Charr urged his cousin, Easurk Charr, to attend school in Riverside and promised to take care of everything else. "So, for the first time in my three years in America I went to school, to the Irving School located at the east end of Fourteenth Street, a couple of blocks away from the Korean camp. Miss Patterson, one of our night school teachers, was the gracious principal of this grade school. There were already two Korean children in the school, a boy and a girl."[30] The girl was Mary Paik Lee, who wrote her biography, *Quiet Odyssey*.

The *Sinhan Minbo* wrote several stories on students at Pachappa Camp including stories about Korean students attending school and learning Chinese characters. Eui Suk Charr, Yong Chan Kim, Bo Pae Lim, Myung Sun Paik, Kwangsun Paik, Jang Son Chun, and Jin Oh Yoon are attending elementary school in Riverside.[31] Eui Suk Charr was Chung Suk Charr's cousin. Yong Chan Kim was the daughter of In Soo Kim. Bo Pae Lim is Joon Ki Lim's daughter. Kwang Sun and Myung Sun Paik were Sin Koo Paik's daughters. Jin Oh Yoon studied Chinese characters at night school. In Soo Kim's daughter Dolly Kim attended the first grade in October 1913, and Nak Chung Thun's nephews, Kyung Moo Thun and Kyung Yoo Thun, entered first and second grades.[32] Yong Chan Kim (son of In Soo Kim) graduated from Junior High School in 1916 and planned to in major economics.[33] The *Sinhan Minbo* reported that five male and four female students attended school in Riverside. "Chang Man Kim sixth grade, Oh Bae Chun fourth grade, Samson Kim third grade, Dolly Kim third grade, William Lee first grade (all Grand public school), Samson Chun Lowell elementary school third grade, Soon Hee Lee Lincoln elementary school first grade, Molly Kim Lincoln elementary school 1st grade, Elizabeth Chun Lincoln elementary school 1st grade."[34] In addition, Choong Sup Park's younger brother Young Sup Park studied electric and carpentry at Junior High School and doing very well.[35]

Going to American schools posed a cultural issue for some of the Korean children who were embarrassed to eat rice and Kimchee lunch boxes at school. "At Pachappa Camp, children hid their buckets and picked them up and ate the food on their way home. The boys had taken to coming home for lunch instead of being embarrassed at school."[36] The Riverside school that the Korean children attended was mostly populated by white students and the rest were an equal number of Mexicans and Asians. Korean children faced overt racial discrimination and often the subject of racial harassment. While attending elementary school in Riverside, Mary Paik Lee recalled how students sang, "Ching Chong Chinaman, Sitting on a wall. Along came a white man, and chopped his head off."[37] The students would then touch Mary's neck and pretend to cut her head off as well. Jacob Thun also experienced similar racial harassment.

> They were excitedly chasing one another when a few big fellows came into their area, clapping and singing, 'Ching, ching, Chinaman, sitting on a rail . . .'[38] They went into action. Hey! Hey! Jap! Jap! Which was like waving a red flag in front of a charging bull. Jacob charged. As he did so, a fellow behind him tackled in a flying leap, sending Jacob sprawling, face down, to the ground.[39] Uncle told Jacob not to back down and stand up for your rights. 'I accept your word. You were not on the winning side. That is lesson enough for today. Next time, strike first.'[40]

The *Riverside Daily Press* reported another racist attack in an article titled "Villainous Spite Work":

> One of the most despicable bits of criminal spite work which has come to light for some time was uncovered this morning, when five Korean boys brought their bicycles Bryan Bros shop with the tires literally slashed to pieces. The tires on the five wheels were worth fully $35, and they have been cut beyond possible repair with great knife gashes. It was evidently work of some sneaking hobo with an imaginary wrong against Koreans and Japanese, or some low-minded orange picker out of job for some cause or another. The Koreans are working for F. D. Lewis on the F. M. Tutin ranch.[41]

Despite the racial discrimination, children were required to attend *Hakyo* (Korean school) and learn and take pride in their Korean heritiage. Ellen Thun wrote, "So boys and girls knew they were Koreans, their parents were Koreans, and that the Japanese—those terrible *waenom* (Japanese) people— had marched into the capital, taken the king the palace, and ousted them."[42] Korean parents made sure that their children grew up with anti-Japanese sentiment. Korean parents often said, "We know what we would do to the *waenoms* and clenched their fists to strike down and hated enemy. Our small children's eyes grew wide, our mouths opened, our hands made into fists, and we looked at one another."[43] Dosan Ahn Chang Ho often spoke to children in a strong stern voice and told the young ones, "Be ready, prepare yourself for the coming independence fight for our country! We will all be in the forefront of battle against the enemy! Carry yourself like Korean patriots! Study hard! Each one be a representative of our nation! Let your actions show you are worthy and a Christian at all times."[44] Korean children at Pachappa Camp grew up learning to be patriot Koreans and prepare themselves to serve their mother country—Nara-il (to serve the nation). Ellen Thun vividly recalled how children at *Hakyo* practiced Korean nationalism.

The children in the *Hakyo* class waited for the teacher. They could hardly sit still. Mr. Choy appeared, cheering, "Manse! Manse!" and the students cried after him, "Manse!" because they knew why he was happy. They were happy, too. The independence of Korea had been declared in the streets of Seoul. Thousands and thousands of students were marching, waving copies of the precious Korean document, unfurling the Korean flag, singing the Korean National Anthem."[45]

Although the Korean National Association Riverside chapter relocated to Vine Street in 1918, the Pachappa Korean community maintained the Korean language school.[46] The *Sinhan Minbo* (September 30, 1920) printed a photo of nine girls, four boys, and two teachers at the Riverside Korean language school. It also reported that thirteen students attended Korean school, and classes would continue until August 27, 1920.[47] According to Ellen Thun, the instructor was Mr. Choy who met Dosan Ahn Chang Ho in Pyongyang. Ahn told him to get a western education to help the country survive in the modern world. Thus, he came to Riverside and became a teacher of the Korean language school. He also worked as an orange picker and learned English to prepare for college. Ellen Thun wrote about Mr. Choy.

He had taught the children Mr. Ahn's song, telling them, 'The song has a secret meaning. But all learned the song. Mr. Song sat back with relief when the children's voices began clear and strong, with Mr. Choy waving the stick leading them: Young men of spirit, standing ready, Bodies of steel, muscles, and bones, it is time for action! Train as though you are face to face with the foe Make victory last forever! Enter the arena as though you are fighting in battle. The gate of victory opens. Beat the drum! Bong! Beat the drum! Bong! Beat the drums of victory! Bong! Bong! Bong! Bong!'[48]

The *Sinhan Minbo* reported that the principal of the Korean school was Il Woo Park, teacher Jae Duk Choi, and the treasurer was In Young Chung.[49] Therefore, it seems reasonable to assume the Mr. Choi that Ellen Thun remembered was probably Jae Duk Choi. He was deacon of the Riverside Korean mission in 1915 and served as vice president and manager of the Riverside chapter of the Korean National Association since 1916. During the anniversary of the Korean National Association foundation day celebration in 1918, he played a violin.

As of 1918, the *Hakyo* at Riverside consisted of three classes (A, B, C) with fourteen students and summer classes began on June 21.[50] In 1920, Korean community leaders discussed plans to open a summer school session to teach Korean, Korean history, and geography to students in either Riverside or Los Angeles. The Korean National Association agreed to provide financial support.

Korean National Association of North America meeting was held in San Francisco between late December 1919 and early January 1920. Delegates discussed the plan to establish three summer schools to teach Korean language either in Riverside or Los Angeles, Dinuba and Sacramento. Local chapters will provide financial support by raising fund locally. Students will learn Korean language, history, and geography.[51]

Riverside was chosen over Los Angeles to open summer school. "Korean language school opened until August 27 in Riverside. A total of thirteen students attended three classes and learned subjects."[52] Interestingly, the *Sinhan Minbo* reported three students graduated with honor and they moved from Riverside to Los Angeles.

Three students attending Polytechnic middle school graduated with honor. First, eldest son of Choong Sup Park, Woon Hak graduated with Suma Cum Laude. In addition, Ji Young Chung's eldest son John and Nak Chung Thun's fourth son Ormias graduated with Cum Laude. Ormias especially is good in Math and he and John has been accepted to one of the best engineering school California Technical College. Cal Tech is the best university in America and only top students receive admission. We are very proud of John and Ormias who have been admitted to the best engineering college in America—Cal Tech.[53]

Jacob Dunn graduated from the University of Michigan and was fluent in English and was an eloquent orator. He was invited by the American Presbyterian Church in Dinuba to speak on the topic of church and politics. Approximately three hundred Korean and Americans attended to listen to the forty-five-minute speech.[54]

NOTABLE KOREAN AMERICANS

Several second-generation Korean American students distinguished themselves in many fields of American society. Young Oak Kim was born on 1919 in Los Angeles. He served as an officer and leader of the famous 100th battalion, which consisted mostly of second-generation Japanese Americans. He and his men fought in Italy and France and became the most decorated unit during World War II. He was honorably discharged in 1946. However, he reenlisted in the U.S. Army when he heard war broke out on the Korean peninsula. He and his unit fought on the Central front and were responsible for moving the Demilitarized Zone forty miles north. He received twenty medals including the second highest military decoration, the Distinguished Service Cross. He was honorably discharged in 1972 as a colonel. As he promised to himself during combat that, "If I survive this war, I will devote my life to the betterment of the community I belong to," he dedicated the rest of his life to humanitarian efforts including fighting for rights of minorities, women, children, adoptees, orphans, and immigrants. He is not only a war hero but more importantly a humanitarian; he passed away in 2005 in Los Angeles. However, he is buried at the national cemetery in Hawaii (Punch Bowl) to be with mostly-Japanese American soldiers from Hawaii who fought with him during World War II.

Dr. Sammy Lee (1920–2016), became the first Asian American to win Olympic gold for the United States in 1948 during the London games. Born in Fresno, California, Dr. Lee's parents owned a chop suey restaurant in Los Angeles. Dr. Lee grew up in the Los Angeles area and was good friends with Young Oak Kim. Dr. Lee was inspired to become a diver after seeing signs for the 1932 Olympic Games posted all over Los Angeles. Dr. Lee pursued his dream with a passion and became a champion diver. He practiced diving at a local pool once a week because it was closed to minorities the rest of the time. The pool water was drained and refilled after the open day for minorities. Thus, Dr. Lee was forced to train on his own. So, he dug a hole in his backyard, filled it with soft dirt, and continued to practice. Ironically, it was later discovered that the water was never drained after the open-minority day. The pool owner claimed to drain the water in order to appease his white swimmers. Rising above discrimination and obstacles, Dr. Lee became a national champion diver and he won gold again at the 1952 Helsinki Olympic Games. Dr. Lee earned his medical degree from the University of Southern California. He also served in the U.S. Army for thirteen years and attained the rank of major. Dr. Lee won several awards for his diving including the Amateur Athletic Union's James E. Sullivan Award.[55]

Philip Ahn, eldest son of Korean independence fighter Ahn Chang Ho, served as the "man of the house" during his father's prolonged absence and paid dearly to keep the family together. Ironically, it was his drive to embrace this "man of the house" role that would eventually spur a career full of roles played out on the silver screen. Philip's name is etched on the sidewalk at 6207 Hollywood Boulevard, on the famous Hollywood Walk of Fame. He has been revered as a pathfinder for the generations of Asian actors and actresses who have followed in his footsteps to filmland. He starred in over two hundred films and television programs, including hits such as "The General Died at Dawn," "The Good Earth," "Battle Hymn," "Love Is a Many-Splendored Thing" and the "Kung Fu" series, in which he played the role of Master Kan. He played his share of stereotypical "Oriental" parts, too, including demonic Japanese military generals and subservient Chinese houseboys.[56]

The early Korean immigrants invested heavily in the education of their children by not only sending them to public schools but also by establishing the *Hakyo* to teach them Korean language, history, and culture. Many students successfully graduated from top universities and became doctors, engineers, scientists, soldiers, and movie stars. During World War II, many Korean young men enlisted in the U.S. Army, Navy, and Air Force and several lost their lives during combat. These young men believed that they were contributing to the independence of Korea by enlisting in the U.S. military during World War II. Finally, Korea became an independent nation when Japan declared unconditional surrender to the Allied Forces on August 15, 1945.

NOTES

1. *Riverside Enterprise,* December 8, 1907.

2. *Riverside Enterprise,* Section Four, Pages 23–30, Sunday Morning, December 8, 1907, No. 65

3. *Annual Report of the Board of Home Missions of the Presbyterian Church in the U.S.A.* (Presbyterian Church in the U.S.A.: 1918), 178.

4. Charr, 1961: 151.

5. Soon Hak Kim provided a wedding invitation, stating a wedding reception between was to be held at 1532 Pachappa Ave on August 7, 1915, at 7:30 p.m. between the couple. Mr. Soon Hak Kim (1876–1919) passed away four years later in 1919, and he was buried at Evergreen Cemetery in Riverside. Riverside Evergreen cemetery document and photo.

6. Personal collection of Mr. Woonha Park. His family lived in Riverside between 1907–1908.

7. Letters and Reports of the Korean Mission, the Board of Foreign Missions, the Presbyterian Church in USA (Presbyterian Historical Society, microfilm #281, Vol. 236, #94) August 1, 1906.

8. *Ibid*, December 31, 1906.

9. Charr, 1961: 70–71.

10. *Sinhan Minbo*, April 14, 1909.

11. Charr, 1961: 71.

12. Transcription of: Letter from Mrs. David Swims to Mrs. Helen Ahn, Los Angeles 31 Jan. 1912. USC Korean Digital Archive.

13. *Sinhan Minbo*, April 28, 1909.

14. *Sinhan Minbo*, July 15, 1920.

15. I received a bible, hymn, photos and other items from Violet Kim in March 2018 a month before she passed away on April 23, 2018.

16. Calvary Presbyterian Church Minutes of Session. Inside the book it says on the cover page: Minutes of the Session of the Presbyterian Church, Presbyterian Board of Publication, No. 1334 Chestnut Street, Philadelphia. Date Range: 6/19/1887–4/2/1906: p. 265 and 267.

17. *Sinhan Minbo*, April 22, 1915.

18. *Sinhan Minbo*, April 22, 1915. It is unclear if this is correct spelling of Reverend Roklin since *Sinhan Minbo* may have wrote his name as it is pronounced in Korean. His name could be Laughlin but not sure.

19. *Sinhan Minbo*, April 29, 1915.

20. *Sinhan Minbo*, April 18, 1918.

21. Charr, 1961: 151.

22. *Gongnip Sinbo*, December 6, 1905.

23. Charr, 1961: 152.

24. Ellen Thun, "Heartwarmers: The New School at West Riverside." Korea Times. October 29, 1996: 14.

25. *Gongnip Sinbo*, June 10, 1908.

26. *Gongnip Sinbo*, October 22, 1906.

27. *Gongnip Sinbo*, January 12, 1907.

28. *Gongnip Sinbo*, February 20, 1907.

29. *Gongnip Sinbo*, April 26, 1907.

30. Charr, 1961: 154.

31. *Sinhan Minbo*, January 12, 1910.

32. *Sinhan Minbo*, October 31, 1913.

33. *Sinhan Minbo*, June 22, 1916.

34. *Sinhan Minbo*, June 21, 1917.

35. *Sinhan Minbo*, October 4, 1923.

36. *Ibid.*

37. Lee, *Quiet Odyssey,* 17.

38. Elen Thun, "Heartwarmers: The New School at West Riverside" Korea Times. August 31, 1996: 10.

39. *Ibid.*

40. *Ibid.*

41. *Riverside Daily Press*, January 6, 1906.

42. Ellen Thun, "Heartwarmers" Korea Times. December 9, 1994.

43. *Ibid.*

44. *Ibid.*

45. Ellen Thun, "Heartwarmers" Korea Times. March 1, 1995: 3.

46. *Sinhan Minbo* reported that Riverside chapter of Korean National Association relocated from 1532 Pachappa Avenue to 1158 Vine Street on November 10, 1918.

47. *Sinhan Minbo*, September 16, 1920.

48. Ellen Thun, Heartwarmers: Annexation. Korea Times. January 28, 1997: 14.

49. *Sinhan Minbo*, April 18, 1918.

50. *Sinhan Minbo*, July 4, 1918.

51. *Sinhan Minbo*, May 18, 1920.

52. *Sinhan Minbo*, September 16, 1920.

53. *Sinhan Minbo*, July 5, 1934.

54. *Sinhan Minbo*, April 16, 1925.

55. Edward T. Chang and Carol Park, *Korean Americans: A Concise History.* Young Oak Kim Center for Korean American Studies, UC Riverside, 2019: 48–49.

56. Edward T. Chang translated, *Lonesome Journey.* Korea University Press, 2016: 155–166.

Chapter Four

Pachappa Families

Unlike other Korean places, Pachappa Camp was a family-based community with women and children. According to the 1910 U.S. Census report, twenty-four Korean families resided at Pachappa Camp: sixteen family-based households and six bachelor households, and sixty-two males and thirty-nine females. One household consisted of children and a non-Korean caretaker. The children of Nak Chung Thun were under the care of Jennie A Wilkins, fifty-seven. His children were: Elizabeth Thun, nine, Ellen Thun, seven, Jack Thun, Amos Thun, three, Esau Thun, one. At the time, Nak Chung Thun and his wife must have temporarily relocated to a nearby place to find work, thus leaving their children with the caretaker.

Pachappa Camp functioned as a base camp for Korean immigrants, and they frequently worked at nearby locations such as Redlands, Upland, and Claremont, and returned to Riverside after their temporary jobs were done. The total number of Korean households decreased to nine, and only forty Korean residents remained at Pachappa Camp according to a 1920 Census report. In this chapter, we trace and reconstruct the family trees of several Korean immigrants who played vital roles in the construction and maintenance of the first Koreatown, Pachappa Camp at Riverside, California. *Gongnip Sinbo* and *Sinhan Minbo* reports and advertisements, along with Ellen Thun's writing and Easurk Emsen Charr's book *The Golden Mountain*, were important sources for understanding the construction of Pachappa families, community, and their activities.

Nin (read like In) Soo Kim and his eldest son Yong Nun Kim played a major role in the construction and maintenance of Pachappa Camp when it was first being established. In Soo Kim was a distant relative of Helen Ahn and helped greatly during Ahn Chang Ho's absence. Yong Nun Kim never left Riverside and his youngest daughter Violet Kim passed away on April 23,

2018, in Riverside; her death ended any direct living links to Pachappa Camp. Soon Hak Kim served as a pastor of the Korean mission and an important member of the Korean National Association and Young Korean Academy. He was killed in a buggy accident in 1919 while working as a baker at the Glenn Mission Inn. His son Tae Sun Kim passed away in 1925 due to cancer.

Nak Chung Thun's family left a prolific amount of written records including diaries, letters, and more. The writings were in both the Korean and English languages and provided invaluable materials which illuminated the early settlement and activities of the Korean families who lived at Pachappa Camp. Nak Chung Thun wrote several novels and stories in Korean and donated them to the USC East Asian library. Ellen Thun published "Heartwarmers" in the *Korea Times* newspaper during the 1990s; the articles provided vivid memories of Pachappa Camp. Nak Chung Thun's nephews Jacob lived with his uncle at Pachappa Camp to continue their education while his parents lived and worked in Hawaii. Unfortunately, Jung Suk Charr and his wife did not have children but attended the Korean mission and were active in the independence movement at Pachappa Camp. Sin Koo Paik and Kuang Do Son had seven sons and three daughters. The eldest daughter, Mary Paik Lee, published "Quiet Odyssey" and wrote about her life at Pachappa Camp as well. Choong Sup Park and his brother Young Sup Park were important members of Pachappa Camp. Their sister, Ae Je Park, married Jung Sup Koo, and they all lived at Pachappa Camp together. Later, Woon Kyung Lee's family carried on the spirit of Pachappa Camp at nearby Vine Street.

NIN SOO KIM FAMILY

Nin (In) Soo Kim—Mary Lee Kim
  (Young Soon Her) (9/17/1867–
  4/23/1959)
(distant relative of Helen Ahn)

Yong Nun Kim (11/7/1886–
  5/31/1954, Riverside)—Hazel Kim
  (9/27/1889–6/14/1978)
(eldest son of In Soo Kim)

Yong Nun Kim (eldest son)
Yong Chan Kim
Dollie Kim (eldest daughter)—
Jung Il Kim (son-in-law)
Nora Kim

Samson Kim (4/7/1908–4/14/1955
  at Delano, Ca)
Mallie Kim
Johnney Kim
Lucy Kim
Violet Kim (–2018)

Nin Soo Kim was a distant relative of Helen Ahn and served as labor contractor at Pachappa. He and his eldest son Yong Nun Kim played major roles in establishing, maintaining, and enhancing Pachappa Camp activities during the early period. In 1915, the mother of Nin Soo Kim's wife passed away in Korea.[1] Nin Soo Kim had two sons and two daughters: Yong Nun, Yong Chan, Dolly, and Nora. Nin Soo Kim passed away in 1949, and his wife Mary Lee Kim died in 1959. The second son, Yong Chan Kim, died in 1925. Nora Kim passed away in 1935. Yong Nun Kim died in 1954. The youngest daughter of Yong Nun and Hazel Kim, Violet Catherine Kim, passed away on April 23, 2018. They are all buried in Olivewood Cemetery in Riverside. According to Ralph Ahn, none of Yong Nun and Hazel Kim's children married except John Kim.

Nin Soo Kim lived and worked in Riverside between 1905 and 1909. He briefly relocated to Logan, Nevada, and returned to Riverside in 1910. Nin Soo and his son Yong Nun Kim were key in helping to build and maintain the early Pachappa Camp Korean community in Riverside. Later, Nin Soo Kim moved to Delano in Northern California to farm. Nin Soo Kim first worked as a labor contractor for the Korean Labor Bureau and recruited Korean workers during orange picking season. According to a *Gongnip Sinbo* advertisement, "Nin Soo Kim is looking for one hundred men to pick orange in Riverside. Workers will receive $1.17 per day."[2] Nin Soo Kim also was elected as president of Riverside chapter of the *Gongnip Hyophoe* (Cooperative Association) in 1905. While Nin Soo Kim served as the president of the Riverside chapter Cooperative Association, he held a "welcoming reception" for Dosan Ahn Chang Ho."[3] In addition, the *Gongnip Sinbo* reported that "60 members in Riverside are working hard, diligent, and active under the leadership of Nin Soo Kim."[4] Nin Soo Kim along with Nak Chung Thun and Chi Wan Lee suggested Korean Americans send representatives to the 2nd World Peace Conference held at the Hague in the Netherlands, but it was too late.[5] Nin Soo Kim continued to work as a labor contractor in 1907 and actively recruited Korean laborers.[6] He also served as chair of judicial affairs and trustee of the Riverside chapter of the Cooperative Association in 1909.[7] He was also philanthropic and donated $5 to the Claremont Student Education Center.[8] Yong Nun and Nin Soo Kim donated $5 and $1 to support the *Sinhan Minbo*, which was facing financial difficulties in 1909.[9] Eng Kyu Kim was appointed as labor contractor for the Riverside Korean Labor Bureau in 1909 when Nin Soo Kim left to farm in Logan, Nevada for a short period.[10] Riverside chapter president Jung Suk Cha sent a letter to the headquarters of the Korean National Association of North America requesting a replacement person for Nin Soo Kim. The situation posed a serious issue for the Riverside Korean Labor Bureau when Nin Soo Kim left to Nevada to farm.[11] In addition, Jin Oh Yoon had to take over the trustee and judicial affairs positions for Nin Soo Kim. Yoon decided to use Nin Soo Kim's residence as the Korean National Association Riverside chapter's building, and he continued to recruit Korean laborers until a new labor contractor was appointed.[12]

Nin Soo Kim returned to Riverside sometime in 1910. As of October 1910, Nin Soo Kim's family also returned to Riverside and tried to bolster the Riverside Korean community.[13] Nin Soo Kim again began to work as labor contractor for the Korean Labor Bureau and actively recruited Korean workers to pick oranges in Riverside.[14] "Orange picking work is not difficult and nearby residence therefor do not need to ride bicycle to work. Workers will receive 20 cents an hour and it will begin early December."[15] The *Sinhan Minbo* (June 7, 1911) reported that "50–60 Korean laborers are picking oranges in Riverside under Nin Soo Kim. Nin Soo Kim also paid off house payment in 1911."[16] Nin Soo Kim was also appointed the welcoming committee delegate during the 1911 Korean National Association of North America convention held in Riverside.[17]

It appears that Nin Soo Kim left Riverside for central California sometime in 1912. He was one of several members who initiated the North American KNA conference in 1911. He also farmed potato fields in Stockton, California; melons in Logan, Nevada; as well as rice in Northern California. And yet, his family continued to reside and work in Riverside. Before he left to central California in 1912, Nin Soo Kim along with Ahn Chang Ho established the North American Industrial Company in order to generate profits and stable income for the Korean American community. The North American Industrial Company intended to raise $45,000 from the Korean American community and placed an advertisement in the *Sinhan Minbo* asking for investors to purchase stocks. Nin Soo Kim served as treasurer of the newly established North American Industrial Company.[18] Ki Man Kim also served as treasurer and he also lived and worked at Pachappa Camp.[19]

By 1913, Nin Soo Kim was fully entrenched in his potato farm in Stockton, California and profited very well; he sold potatoes for $1 a box.[20] But then, Nin Soo Kim decided to return to Logan, Nevada, where he had briefly farmed in 1909, with thirteen other Korean immigrants and leased 188 acres to grow melon sometime in 1915.[21] He continued to grow melon at Logan, Nevada until the summer of 1918. Nin Soo Kim left Nevada in 1918 and leased two hundred acres of land to grow rice in Northern California along with other Korean farmers such as Chong-lim Kim (who was known as the "rice king"), Young Soon Park, Sin Koo Paik in fall of that year.[22] Nin Soo Kim would later invest in rice farming in Riverside along with two other people in 1918 by providing funds. In 1920, Yong Nun Kim went to Hawaii to start a pineapple farm.[23] He submitted an application to the state of California on April 16, 1920, to gain permission to transact business in Hawaii.

For the past sixteen years he has resided in and still resides in Riverside, California, with his wife and four children, all of the children having been born in Riverside. His mother and two sisters are also residents of Riverside, and his father is engaged in business in Willows, California. He makes this affidavit in order to show and establish the fact that he is and has been a resident of California for over sixteen years so that he may return to his home and family in Riverside, California, after attending to business affairs in Honolulu.

The reason why he applied for this document is that he was unable to secure Japanese passport when he applied for passport to Japanese Consul and to the Japanese Association. Therefore he had submit affidavit in order to be able to return from Hawaii to California. He was granted permission and expires on December 24, 1922.[24] Yong Nun Kim's youngest daughter kept many notes on life of Yong Nun Kim in Honolulu, Hawaii. Yong Nun Kim continued reside in Riverside along with Woon Kyung Lee and Jung Sup Koo families in 1923.[25]

He would not return to Riverside until sometime in 1921; records in Riverside show that Nin Soo Kim was a resident in the city at the time and he donated $2 a relief fund to help the Kando disaster in China.[26] Finally, Nin Soo Kim purchased a house in Santa Ana in 1922 and left Riverside.[27] Nin Soo Kim resided in Santa Ana, but continued to farm in Delano along with other investors.[28] Yong Nun Kim and Dolly Kim placed an advertisement in the *Sinhan Minbo* inviting people to celebrate their father's sixtieth birthday in Santa Ana. During the ceremony, Helen Ahn gave a speech on behalf of her family.[29] Nin Soo Kim also attended Helen Ahn's sixtieth birthday party in 1944.[30] Nin Soo Kim hurt his rib while carrying a haystack in Delano, California in 1940. He returned to Riverside home (5789 Streeter Avenue, Riverside) to rest.[31] Nin Soo Kim never lost contact with his eldest son Yong Nun Kim and grandchildren who resided and worked in Riverside.

YONG NUN KIM AND SIBLING

Yong Nun Kim took over his father's role as labor contractor when Nin Soo Kim relocated to central California in 1912. He placed an advertisement in the *Sinhan Minbo* to recruit eighty-five to one hundred Korean laborers to pick oranges in Riverside.[32] Workers were paid $2 per day for nine hours of work. Yon Nun Kim's eldest daughter Dollie Kim was a 1st grader who attended elementary school in Riverside in 1913. His second son, Yong Chan Kim, attended Claremont Middle School (second grade) in 1914.[33] In 1917, Nin Soo Kim's eldest daughter Dollie Kim and Yong Nun Kim's eldest son Samson attended Riverside Grand School as third-graders.[34] Mallie Kim was a first-grader. The children of Yong Nun Kim all attended schools in Riverside as well as *Hakyo* between 1918 and 1924. Yong Chan Kim passed away due to an illness in 1925.[35] Dollie Kim married Chester Kim (Jung Il Kim) in 1926. The wedding ceremony was held at Nin Soo Kim's residence in Santa Ana.[36]

SOON HAK AND TAE SUN KIM

Soon Hak Kim—Father
Tae Sun Kim (Son)

Both Soon Hak Kim and his son Tae Sun Kim are buried at Evergreen Cemetery in downtown Riverside. Soon Hak Kim was killed in 1919 in a buggy accident and his son Tae Sun Kim died of cancer in 1925. Soon Hak Kim's headstone is written in Korean which states he was a member of both the Korean National Association and the Young Korean Academy. He served as interim president of the Riverside chapter of the Korean National Association of North America during its convention held in Riverside in 1911. Soon Hak Kim also served as a pastor of the Korean mission during its early years. Soon Hak Kim arrived in Hawaii at the age of twenty-nine on October 12, 1904. Despite his struggles, Soon Hak Kim donated $1 to help with the *Gongnip Hyophoe* fund in early 1907.[37] Based on newspaper articles, he came to Riverside sometime before May 1907. Soon Hak Kim officially joined the *Gongnip Hyophoe* Riverside chapter in June 1907.[38] Between 1911 and 1914, Soon Hak Kim played a prominent role in institutionalizing the Pachappa Camp community as president and vice president of the Riverside Chapter of the Korean National Association of North America. He continued to serve an important role as a judicial affairs officer in 1916 and as a representative in 1917.[39] He also invested in rice farming in Willows, California, along with Jung Hee Maeing in 1916; they made a net profit of $1,113.[40] Soon Hak Kim delivered a key note speech during a National Humiliation Day ceremony in Riverside on August 29, 1917.[41] He also gave a speech on the "History of Riverside Korean National Association" during the Korean National Association anniversary day ceremony in 1918.[42] His son Tae Sun Kim sang a song during the same ceremony. Soon Hak Kim continued to actively serve the Riverside Korean community until he was killed in a buggy accident in 1919.

NAK CHUNG THUN FAMILY

Chai Soo Chun

Nak Choon Dunn—Sim Eun   Nak Chung Thun—Ruth (Ru)
(eldest son)   (second son)

Frank (Kyung Bu) Dunn
Jacob (Kyung Mu) Dunn (1899)
John (Kyung Yu) Dunn
5 more children

Obed Thun (1906)
Samson Thun (1908)
Elizabeth (1910)
Ellen Thun (1912)—twin sister still born
Jack Thun (1914)
Amos Thun
Arthur Thun (1918)

Chai Soo Chun was the father of Nak Choon Dunn and Nak Chung Thun. For unknown reasons, the two boys changed the spelling of their surname. Nak Chung and Ruth were the parents of Ellen Thun. Nak Chung Thun was born in 1880 and raised as sort of a small village scholar in Jeongju, North Korea. Ellen Thun recalls her father telling her about his home town: "It's the dispatch saying American bombers bombed Korean industrial city by the name of Jeongju, and my father said that was our village a long time ago."[43] Nak Chung Thun (twenty-four) with his wife Ruth (nineteen), his father Chai Soo Chun (fifty), his brother Nak Choon (thirty-four) and Nak's wife Pak Si (twenty-eight), and Thun's two sons Frank and Jacob arrived in Hawaii on March 4, 1904. They departed from Kobe, Japan on February 21, 1904.[44] Another Korean man named Nak Won Chun (twenty-four) also came to Hawaii on the same ship. It is unclear if he is related to or was the twin brother of Nak Chung Thun since they were the same age. On the ship Korean and Japanese children played together because they were bored but parents didn't discourage it. A woman on board of the ship the Thun's were also traveling on—the *S.S. Siberia 2*—gave birth to a baby girl. They named her Siberia Kim."[45]

It is not clear when the two brothers (Nak Chung and Nak Choon) decided to change their last names from Chun to Thun and Dunn. Nak Chung and his wife had five sons and three daughters (Ellen's twin sister was still born).[46] Nak Chun Thun's eldest son Obed was born in Kauai in 1906. His other children were all born in Riverside, including Sam in 1908, Elizabeth in 1910, Ellen in 1912, Jack in 1914, and the youngest Arthur was born in 1918. According to Ellen, her father named everyone from the Bible except Ellen. "Obed was the son of Ruth in the Bible. My father named everybody from the Bible you know except me. Jacob named me. He was graduating from grammar school and he read about an Ellen in Scott's *Lady of the Lake*. So, he decided and asked my father, 'Can I name her Ellen?' and my father said go ahead. He didn't care."[47]

Nak Choon and his father Chai Soo lived and worked in Hawaii. As of 1906, Nak Chung Thun, his parents and his brother were residing in Hawaii. According to the *Gongnip Sinbo* (September 7, 1906), "Nak Chung Thun and Jae Sang Han, residents of Kaui, sent $4 to Education Affairs of *Gongnip*

Hyophoe to support students. Nak Chung Thun and his family relocated to Riverside around 1907 and was elected as vice president of the Riverside chapter of *Gongnip Hyophoe* in 1908."[48] According to Ellen Thun, her parents came to Riverside with two nephews because of her uncle, Nak Choon. "He was a very unusual man. Uh, he was the oldest, but he admired my father because he always thought my father was so brainy. And he was the one who really encouraged my father all the time to study and you know to learn everything if you can. My uncle didn't have as much as education because they were having to work the farm all the time, but my father would help on the farm but he was allowed to go to the village school until there's no more school there."[49] Before Nak Chung Thun's family settled in Riverside, they were railroad construction workers in the Mojave Desert. When they came from the Mojave Desert to Riverside, Nak Chung's nephew Jacob declared, "It was so wonderful to come into a town that had nothing but orange grows. The deserts had been so bleak and bear, and here they come into the area of miles and miles of orange growths—looks like heaven to them."[50]

Nak Chung Thun's wife Ruth gave birth to their last son Isaac on February 5, 1918.[51] Ruth was unwell and suffered from a mental illness. Ruth would self-inflict wounds all over her body with a hammer and shards of glass.[52] She was not active in Korean National Association activities either. Ellen recounted what she heard about her mother.

> She only came to the meeting when she still had silk dresses from Korea. Then, there was no money for silk dresses; she never came to our meetings. Poor thing. But, she meant that my mother had too much pride. But, the thing was by that time all that was happening with the meeting, my mother had too many children and she had to stay home to take care of the children you know [one] right after the other. And this was something I know that my cousin Jacob felt that my father was very wrong and having so many children because after I was born, the doctor was very concerned about my mother's mental health.[53]

Ruth ended up committing suicide, and the children were placed at the Riverside County Children's Home. "When news of the tragic ending to *Sam-il* (March 1) Day came to them, Mrs. Chun asked Mr. [Choy] that the children learn "Arirang." She seldom had shown herself in the class. This day they heard her sing. After this occasion, Mrs. Chun retired into her own private asylum, over the mountain, and would not return. She attempted suicide a few months later and was hospitalized."[54] According to Ellen, Obed was ashamed and angry at their mother. "And so, Obed was so angry at my mother after her death for trying to commit suicide and it was in the paper that he was ashamed to go to school. So, he was in the eighth grade and he never went back to school. But you know he was very smart."[55] Obed was traumatized by his mother's suicide and he never married. Ellen Thun described Obed's love life:

> Obed never married because he was out in Hawaii for a while. *Gwa-Bu*'s (widows), they were mad to marry him because he told me later that he spoke the most beautiful Korean. [The widows] never heard [an] overseas Korean be such a high class and they wanted [a] husband [that was] a high class Korean as well. I didn't know what high class Korean was, but he said high class. But he said to me that he didn't like responsibilities because he never got over my mother's suicide. I think he hated all women for that, of course it was psychological, and probably I'm wrong but all I know all my life is that he sure hates women. So, it wasn't surprising at all that he never married.[56]

Ellen's second oldest brother, Samson, married a Korean woman named Alice. Her other brothers married white women. Ellen's siblings got government jobs working, not high paying positions, but good enough, she said. They made enough money to buy homes and support their wives and children and had cars. When they retired, there was enough money to keep their homes.

Nak Chung Thun and Ruth's five youngest children, who were under nine years of age, were placed in the Riverside County Children's Home, an American orphanage. Ellen Thun recalls her time at the orphanage: "They were kind to us; they took care of us. It was our first time having plenty of food, clothes, they weren't always new, but my father would sometimes send money and they would buy us yardage and they would make up clothes."[57] However, they faced the harsh reality of racism as they were trained to become house workers for the two girls and the boys were taught agricultural work, according to Ellen. So, the boys learned how to work in the garden, take care of the cows, goats, and chickens. "In the meantime, Mr. Thun continued scrubbing pots and pans at the cafeteria to make a living."[58] When the news of Mrs. Thun's suicide attempt spread, the Korean community fundraised to help the Thun family. The seven children were placed in the care of a local orphanage because Nak Chung and Ruth Thun couldn't take care of them. According to a 1920 U.S. Census report, they resided at 923 Lemon Street in Riverside. Nak Chung Thun's household: husband and wife, five sons and two daughters: Nak A Thun (forty-two), Ruth (thirty-four), Obed (fourteen), Samson (eleven), Elizabeth (nine), Ellen (seven), Jack (five), Amos who was recorded as Ormias (four), Arthur who was recorded as Isaac (one). It is not clear why names of Amos and Arthur was recorded with different spelling.

The children of Nak Chung Thun attended local public school and *Hakyo* which was Korean language school. According to Ellen, her life was a little different from her sister's.

Elizabeth was nine and she had been to school already, but I didn't go to school on time. I was at home. They didn't have clothes for me, therefore, I never [went] to school [on] weekdays. But my sister had been going to school for three or almost four years and she never liked. I meant she liked the school and learning but she was isolated. She went to all American school. There was a mix school for children of other Koreans, Mexicans, and blacks but my father went to this school board to send the children to segregated school. He just told them they couldn't, he said, 'we came to America to become educated.' And they liked that so they told him Obed and Sam can go to this English school just for Americans. A few Japanese and eventually other smart Koreans were tested and were allowed to go too. I think they were the first Oriental kids who went to English school and they did very well. Obed was so smart, the first school he went to had an IQ test and he scored way up at the top you know. And later the same woman came down at the army for where I went to grammar school to give me the test and she said, 'Are you Obed's sister?' I said yes, and she shook her head and said, 'Well, we don't have to worry about you.' But she gave me this test, it was just pictures I had to identify. That's all it was.[59]

Amos Thun was very good at math and he was admitted to California Technical University in 1934.[60] During World War II, Obed, Samson, Jack, Amos, Arthur—all five of Nak Chun's sons—joined the U.S. military. Jack Thun received the Silver Star and Purple Heart medals.[61] Sam Thun and Alice Whang married on July 17, 1943. At the time, Sam was serving as a second lieutenant in the U.S. Air Force.[62] Alice celebrated her 105th birthday on August 13, 2017, and several months later she passed away. Alice was born at Ewha plantation in Hawaii and moved to Los Angeles when she was eight years old. While attending college, she met Sam at a dance party. The couple married and she worked at the Los Angeles Water and Power department until she retired.

As previously mentioned, Nak Chung Thun wrote four unpublished manuscripts and it includes his family life at Pachappa Camp. According to the *GujejokGangdo* manuscript, Jack Thun returned to Riverside and met with Mrs. Wilkins. As previously mentioned, Nak Chung Thun's children lived in Mrs. Wilkins' household according to the 1910 U.S. Census. The manuscript also includes the story of Jack Thun who returned to Los Angeles after serving in the U.S. military during World War II. The *Sinhan Minbo* (December 10, 1942) also reported that Obed, Amos, Arthur, Sam, and Jack Thun served during World War II. In another manuscript, Nak Chung documented Jack's life and told of how Jack was admitted to Los Angeles high school as a ninth grader in September 1929. However, the *Sinhan Minbo* (December 26, 1929) reported that Jack was an eighth grader in Los Angeles in 1929. In Nak Chung's *Owolwha* manuscript, Jack is described as being very good at mathematics and popular with female students. When Jack was attending high school in Los Angeles, he was disappointed when a girl named Catherine rejected him. He won her over however, by giving up his spot as valedictorian at the *Hakyo* in Riverside to Catherine. She was deeply moved by Jack and invited him to a prom party. Clearly, Nak Chung Thun's writings are based on true stories about his children and he provides vivid descriptions of what early life was like for the Thun family in Riverside and Los Angeles.

During an interview with Ellen, she recounted an interesting story about her father and a doctor that treated the Thun family.

> And so it was just too bad that my father had very superior feelings that women were more like animals, I guess because he didn't take the doctor seriously. And the doctor was friendly enough, he always came and took care of us and never asked to be paid. And he talked to my father about many things and even talked to him and asked, "How did Orientals cope with syphilis?" And my father learned that the doctor's son had contacted syphilis through the prostitute in that area. And those days, syphilis was very serious, and my father told him what the Chinese doctors used. And so the doctor went back to New York to see the Chinese doctors. It was through some Chinese herb or something medication. Anyway, my father said the doctor was very happy and came to him to thank him over and over again for saving his son because those days, men usually died of syphilis.[63]

Nak Chung Thun had strained relations with his sons and nephews. However, he got along well with his two daughters. Ellen recounted their relationship.

> Just only with my sister and me. He would come down for his money because we couldn't give him big sum of money, but we could give him some supplies. We didn't know where he got his clothes from, but his brother and his wife were already living here and I think his brother gave him his old clothes because my father always had a pretty good suit on and shirt that wasn't wrinkly.[64]

Later in life, Nak Chung Thun became very poor and was unable to support himself. Ellen and her brothers took turns giving their father $10 a month. Despite the fact that they earned "peanuts" for a living at the time, Ellen and her sister ended up supporting Nak Chung more than their brothers did over time.

Nak Chung Thun continued to live a difficult life. At times, he was penniless and depended on his children for money. Nak Chung passed away in 1953, according to Ellen.

> He was 83 [when he died]. But, during that time, he was invisible. My brothers had nothing to do with him except accidentally. He moved in with the old Korean grandfathers that a Christian church minister started in a poor town. He rented a place, so that the Korean old men would have a place, they were

homeless really. My father was just like an old homeless man. So, he never complained to me. I know he was ashamed that this happened. He accepted whatever fate he was given. I always felt bad, but I was done and out of money too. I couldn't help him.[65]

NEPHEWS: FRANK AND JACOB DUNN

Nak Chung's nephews, Frank and Jacob Dunn, came to Riverside from Hawaii to continue their education.[66] They lived in Nak Chung Thun's household while attending a local school. As of October 1913, Frank was a first-grader and Jacob was in the second grade in Riverside.[67] "Frank was proud of his younger brother Jacob. In fact [Frank] became a long-job boy because that meant he had a permanent job. He worked from 1908 through till 1913. And that is known as the year of big freeze when the orange grove in Riverside, the temperature dropped down to about 40 degrees in a day and below 32 at night,"[68] Ellen Thun recalled.

Jacob relocated to nearby Claremont to continue his education in 1915 and 1916. However, he was not able to finish middle school as he had to work from April to October. He came back to Riverside with $200 and tried to attend high school again. However, he was three weeks late and not able to attend. When he could finally enroll, Jacob was very angry at his uncle for not being able to attend high school because of the financial hardship Nak Chung Thun was experiencing; they didn't have enough money for school. "I am not getting any education but that is the reason why you brought me to America to get education." Jacob said to his uncle.[69] Jacob's grandfather hoped Jacob would become a leader and told Nak Chung Thun to send Jacob to General Robert E. Lee's college. "Jacob must become a general or at least a military man because Korea is going to have to have fighters."[70]

With the $200 Jacob earned, and with the support from his brother Frank, Jacob was sent to West Virginia to attend college in 1916. He never traveled before and had lots of fun. When he reached Missouri from St. Louis, he decided to stay for a few weeks to see the community and experience life there; he spent all of his money and left with only $10. Stuck with only a small sum in his pocket, Jacob asked the ticket man where he could go for ten dollars. The ticket man replied, " You can get to Louisville for $10 and you will have a quarter left."[71] Jacob checked into the Louisville YMCA and had to earn his living for about a year because school had already started and he wasn't able to enroll. He met a woman named Keller who was an executive secretary of one of the biggest insurance companies in the South, she urged him to "go back to fight for Korea." She told him to live with her and she would provide lodging, food, and financial support while he finished high school.

Jacob decided to take her up on her offer and finished high school in 1919. He then pursued a college degree and earned a scholarship from the University of Michigan and was able to graduate. The Korean community in Riverside was very proud of Jacob for his educational accomplishments. Jacob made name for himself as a great debater while he was in college. He excelled in English, history, and economics but earned C's in math and science classes. Everyone wondered why he majored in English and history and not science or medicine, which is what Korea needed at the time.

When he graduated from the University of Michigan in 1924, he was not able to get a job at a major American corporation and was unable to support himself. He decided to return to Korea in 1925. When he was asked to speak at a big church in Korea, he delivered a lecture in English. The American minister asked, "don't you speak Korean?" Jacob had forgotten his native language and spoke very little Korean. Everyone in Korea wanted to know how he received an education in America. Unable to communicate in Korean, a translator explained that Jacob was able to go to college because he received scholarships and he worked. Jacob found a job teaching English at a Korean university, but he found it very boring. He decided to visit his aunt living in Manchuria. She told him that there is no possibility of building up a major Korean military in Manchuria. Jacob's uncle, Nak Chung Thun, always spoke of building a major military base in Manchuria to gain Korea's independence. Jacob's visit to Manchuria confirmed that there was no way a Korean military base could be built there.

Jacob decided to return to America and went to Hawaii because he was afraid to come to California; he had married a girl in Dinuba. He met Maria Suh in 1925 and married her in three months. The marriage changed the whole trajectory of Jacob's future as a Korean leader, according to Ellen Thun.[72] His parents told Jacob to go back to California due to the bad economic conditions in Hawaii. However, Jacob stayed in Hawaii for a year and finally returned to California at the end of 1927. Jacob finally told Nak Chung Thun that he was married. At the time, Nak Chung was able to bring five of his children home from the orphanage where they had been for five years. Ellen, who was twelve years old, and her sister were put to work in American families. Nak Chung Thun and his five sons along with four of his uncles' children were living in a three-bedroom house. When Jacob and his wife joined them, twelve people had to live in the three-bedroom house, and it was difficult to say the least. Nak Chung Thun's farming efforts failed due to poor weather and the inability to find enough workers during years of good crops.

The Thun family left several unpublished novels and manuscripts both in Korean and English. Ellen Thun read Jacob Dunn's manuscript and wrote a book called "Personal Note." Jacob wrote about his life and his time at the University of Michigan where played football. He also was an orator as he was in charge of speech club. During the first Korean Student Association meeting in 1923, Jacob served as Master of Ceremony and Philip Jaisohn delivered a keynote speech. Jacob was well-known for his public speaking ability in English within Korean immigrant community at the time. After graduation, Jacob worked for Korean independence activities in Washington DC. He married Maria Suh on September 12, 1925. Jacob and Maria's daughter was born in December 1929 in Los Angeles.[73] Jacob wrote a story on the 1932 Summer Olympic Games for the *Sinhan Minbo*.[74] In 1932, he also delivered several lectures on China-Japan relations and on Manchuria and Korea related issues in Chicago; he represented the Korean National Association. Jacob finished his own biography in 1934 or 1935 according to Ellen Thun.[75] He send it to several publishers, but all rejected his manuscript and it was never published. Jacob later returned to Korea and served as vice-chair of the Korean Olympic Committee in 1945. Two years later, he died in a crash onboard a U.S. military airplane. He was on his way to a meeting in Stockholm, Sweden. He was instantly killed along with forty others when it crashed in 1947.[76]

According to Ellen, Frank Dunn suffered major brain damage after being injured during farming accident in 1925. She recounted the incident.

> Frank was then farming somewhere around Dinuba area and he was plowing. When the horse was frightened by something, it was one of those great big wooden plows that turns into soil. And uh the horse ran away and Frank got caught up in a disc, wooden disc. He was caught in that and his hands were all wrapped up in the rain and the horse just went wild. Frank would knock in the head and just caught up that his legs were broken, and his arms were broken before the horse finally stopped. And I guess somehow, someone came by and saw that Frank was just knocked out. They thought he was dead, so they rushed him to hospital. And the doctors were really good. They operated on his brain, but there were so much damage to his brain. He never could think very much, except as a child. Then they took care of his broken arms and legs and it was long time before he was able to work again. But, by that time, he was very child-like and it took a long time before he could work again as a little more adult. But, really, he was always a child.

Jacob and Frank grew up living their lives in different ways. While Jacob pursued education and was a great speaker, Frank became an eccentric, flamboyant person. He was a gambler and wore expensive suits. Initially, Frank obeyed his uncle's orders, but later revolted against his uncle's authoritarian attitude and they had strained relations. Ellen Thun recalled some of her memories of Frank.

> He was always aggressive, he was always farming and making money, but he would not help my father except with a little bit of money because Frank by that

time had become very eccentric, he loved beautiful clothes and liked to gamble. So, he spent you know when he had a farm and made money, it was not just pennies, it might be like in [unintelligible], he made $13,000 in one year. But, he came into Los Angeles and bought tailor made suits like a rich man would and custom made shoes because he had very tender skin and so shoes bothered him. They were expensive. And then when he was all dressed up, of course he got involved with the Chinese, Japanese and Korean gamblers. They would say, 'You are my friend, come with us.' and they made the round of the Stockton gambling hall and Los Angeles had plenty you know. And by the end of December after about maybe four–five months, a lot of money was gone. And he had lots of gold teeth put in and what he would do during gambling was that he would take his tooth out and [unintelligible] for a few dollars. And if he won, he would go back and get his tooth back. I mean this was his mentality, he [unintelligible] in his sophomore year of high school, never understood the American education, never understood what my father wanted them to do or become. He was only angry at my father because when he was about eighteen, there was a Korean family that wanted him to marry their daughter and my father said "Don't marry her. She came from very poor family. No good!" and you know any other young man would go ahead and marry that girl if you really wanted to. But, Frank again like Jacob, they did obey my father for a long time. They thought he was the head of the family. And so, Frank just went off and he and my father were never close again because he was very angry about being told that Korean girls here were not worthy of the Dunn name."

JUNG SUK CHA FAMILY

Jung Suk Cha—Jung Sung   Cha Easurk Charr —Young Sun Charr (Kim)

Jung Suk Cha was active member of the Cooperative Association and the Korean National Association between 1907 and 1913. He served as president of the Riverside chapter of the Cooperative Association and the Korean National Association between 1907 and 1910. He also organized a discussion group and was elected as secretary of the newly formed group. In 1910, Cha was hit by a car and was severely wounded. He was hospitalized, suffered from neck pain, was unable to speak, and barely able to communicate.[77] However, Cha recovered from his injuries and was able to continue his independence activities. In preparation for the 1911 Korean National Association of North America convention, he was appointed as an administrative assistant and attended the convention as the Riverside delegate.[78]

It is unclear why and when Jung Suk Cha moved to Pasadena and away from Riverside. However, he didn't stop supporting the Korean American community nor its fight for the independence of Korea. He implored his fellow Korean immigrants to donate and support the ailing *Sinhan Minbo* in 1917.[79] When the March 1, 1919 nationwide *Mansei* movement in Korea occurred, he wrote a column urging Koreans in Korea and overseas Koreans to unite and declare Korea's national independence.[80] Jung Suk Cha was an active Korean independence movement member and in 1922 he was elected as vice-president of the Los Angeles chapter of the Korean National Association.[81] He continued to donate duty funds and participate in the Korean National Association until 1945.

Jung Suk Cha and his wife Jung Sung Cha did not have children but she maintained close relations with the Cha family members and frequently visited them in San Francisco. When she was living in Pasadena in 1930, she visited San Francisco to meet her siblings.[82] She also provided care for her sister in law for three weeks until she passed away due to illness in 1932.[83] When women were allowed to join the Korean National Association as full members in 1918, she also became very active in the Korean independence movement. She donated $10 to the Korean Patriotic Women's League in 1919.[84] Jung Suk Cha and Jung Sung Cha continued to pay annual duty funds of $10 each, every year. Jung Sung Cha passed away on March 26, 1944 and the *Sinhan Minbo* published a long obituary to commemorate her contributions to the church and the Korean independence movement. "She spent almost half of her life to support church and independence activities in the U.S. She married Jung Suk Cha, but they did not have children of their own. Many attended her funeral services in San Francisco including Helen and Susan Ahn, Nin Soo Kim, Easurk Emsen Charr from Portland, and many others."[85]

Jung Suk Cha and Easurk Emsen Charr were cousins. Charr was interviewed and his life story was recorded by a team of journalists.

When Korea fell under Japan's control in 1905, Easurk Emsen Charr, a twelve-year-old boy from *Pyongyang* province, landed in San Francisco with one burning ambition: to return home as a medical missionary. He had to stop in Hawaii since he didn't have enough money to travel to the Promised Land. To pay back the passage, the boy worked on a sugar plantation for months, for five cents an hour, ten hours a day, six days a week. Upon arriving in San Francisco, he met the legendary Ahn Chang Ho, who would arrange for him a houseboy job, then "white collar jobs" as a busboy and waiter. He would follow Ahn to Riverside, California where he would pick fruit alongside the great patriot and labor organizer. A true believer in the American Dream, Charr would spend a quarter century chronicling his glorious American venture in *The Golden Mountain: The Autobiography of a Korean Immigrant*, leaving out all the pain and hurt of anti-Asian exclusion laws and humiliation that dogged him throughout his extraordinary passage.[86]

In his autobiography *The Golden Mountain*, Easurk Emsen Charr described how he worked at orange farms during picking seasons from Christmas to spring for about ten weeks. When his cousin Jung Suk Cha and his wife Jung Sung Cha arrived in San Francisco in 1906, a massive earthquake hit, and he worried about their safety. Fortunately, they received help and support from Dr. Drew and safely came to Riverside. Easurk Emsen Charr was pushed to continue his education while working and he was active in the Korean independence movement in Riverside. In 1907, he moved to Salt Lake City and continued to study and participate in independence activities.[87] Korean immigrants provided financial support to Easurk Emsen Charr when he was studying in Salt Lake City.[88] He returned to Riverside in 1910 and attended *Hakyo* along with Mary Paik Lee.[89] In 1913, he attended Park College and joined a student association and gave several public lectures on the "current political situation of Korea."[90] He enlisted in the U.S. Army during World War I and was honorably discharged in 1919.[91]

Easurk Emsen Charr married his wife on June 10, 1928, in Chicago. Her maiden name was Young Sun Kim. She came from Euiju, North Korea, and graduated from the prestigious Ewha Women's University in Korea. She majored in nursing and came to America to continue her studies in 1926.[92] Easurk Emsen Charr worked at Rand McNelly and Young Sun continued her education at Duke University and later Kinwoodrowing (Korean pronunciation and unclear exactly where).[93]

SIN KOO PAIK FAMILY

Sin Koo Paik—Kwang Do Paik (Sohn)

Myung Sun Paik
Kwang Sun Paik (Mary Paik Lee)
Do Sun (Earnest) Paik
Kyung Sun (Stanford) Paik
Hong Sun (Arthur) Paik
Neung Sun (Ralph) Paik
Young (Lawrence) Paik
Charlotte Lok Sun Paik
Heh Sun (Edward) Paik
Ock Sun (Florence) Paik

Sin Koo Paik was born on October 6, 1873, in Dang Chu, Korea. He arrived in Honolulu, Hawaii, and his son Ernest Tau Sun was born in Ewa Planation, Oahu on October 6, 1905. He moved from Hawaii to Riverside in 1906, and joined the Riverside chapter of the Korean National Association in April 1909.[94] He was appointed as vice-president and secretary of the Riverside chapter of the Korean National Association immediately after he joined.[95] In addition, he served as education affairs officer of the newly formed discussion group in Riverside. Sin Koo Paik placed an advertisement in the *Sinhan Minbo* (May 12, 1909). He printed forty member names and asked readers if they knew the whereabouts of the individuals and to please contact him. Since many Korean laborers worked as seasonal migratory farm workers at the time, they often joined the KNA and relocated elsewhere if they found jobs in another location. The Riverside chapter of the Korean National Association were probably trying to identify location of the members who were no longer active in Riverside. Sin Koo Paik with Jung Suk Char and Suk Won Lee led a fundraising campaign to purchase the *Sinhan Minbo* building in 1910.[96] He moved to Claremont sometime in 1910 and later served as president of the Claremont chapter of the Korean National Association in 1912. Kwang Do Paik (Sohn) also actively participated in the independence movement and contributed $4 to the Korean Patriotic Women's League in 1919.[97] Both Sin Koo Paik and Kwang Do Paik actively participated in the independence movement by contributing duty funds and other independence donations until Korea gained independence in August 1945.

Sin Koo Paik's family continued to follow the harvests and moved all over California. In 1916, he became a successful rice farmer along with Chong-lim Kim (Rice King). Several Koreans became rice farmers because of their experience in raising the crop. Many of them became successful. Chong-lim Kim farmed 1,030 acres, Young Soon Park farmed 240 acres, Jin Sup Lee farmed 150 acres, Myung Sun Hwang farmed 80 acres, Ji Sung Lim farmed 80 acres, and Sin Koo Paik farmed 75 acres.[98] In 1918, Chong-lim Kim increased his operations and farmed 1,800 acres, and Sin Koo Paik's rice farm increased to 500 acres.[99] During World War I, rice prices skyrocketed because of growing demand. The successful Korean rice farmers contributed some of their earnings to the Korean independence fund. In 1920, Chong-lim Kim donated at least $50,000 to help start the Willows Korean Aviation School/Corps to train pilots to fight against Japan.[100]

Sin Koo Paik and Kwang Do Paik's family was large; they had seven sons and three daughters. The oldest son and daughter, along with other Korean children, attended school in the local Riverside community. According to the KNA Riverside chapter report in 1910, Easurk Charr, Yong Chan Kim, BoPae Lim, Myung Sun Paik, Kwang Sun Paik, Jang Son Chun, and Soja Chun were attending elementary school in Riverside.[101] Sin Koo Paik's eldest son Myung Sun and his eldest daughter Kwang Sun (Mary) were attending elementary school in Riverside. According to Mary Paik Lee, she attended Irving school in Riverside. Five of Paik's sons joined the U.S. military during World War II—Ernest, Arthur, Stanford, and Ralph already enlisted in the U.S. military.[102] Lawrence Young Sun Paik at the age of thirty-five served on the Pacific front as a machine gunnery of airplane and flew 110 times. He enlisted in 1940 and fought in New Guinea. He also fought in the Philippines and earned seven medals.[103] During World War II, more than two hundred young Korean American men and women from the U.S. mainland and several hundred more from Hawaii enlisted in the U.S. Army, Navy, and Air Force. They believed that it helped to liberate Korea from Japanese colonial domination.

Kwang Sun (Mary) Paik married Hong Man Lee on January 1, 1919, in Willows, California.[104] Kwang Sun Paik became Mary Paik Lee and published *Quiet Odyssey: A Pioneer Korean Woman in America* in 1990. Myung Sun Paik married Young Soon Park on February 27, 1929, in Idaho. and Edward Paik married Katherine Lim, the daughter of Reverend Jung Koo Lim, on June 21, 1942.[105] Ralph Paik married Ok Ja Kim in August 1938.[106] Many guest attended the wedding and Jacob Dunn served as the Master of Ceremony.

CHOONG SUP PARK FAMILY

Hong Sik Park—Sang Soon Park

Choong Sup Park— Jung Kyung Park (Lee)	Young Sup Park — Wha Soon Park (Kim)	Ae-Joo Park (Koo)— Jung Sup Koo
Woon Ha Park		Chung Woon (Walter) Koo
Woon Yong Park		Eun Bok (Grace) Koo
Woon Sun Park		Eun Jin (Florence) Koo
In Sook Park		Eun Pyo Koo
		Eun Hye Koo
		Eun Ae Koo

Choong Sup Park came to Riverside from San Francisco sometime in 1907.[107] He along with Dalno Kim and Choon Bong Ma joined the Riverside chapter of the Cooperative Association in June 1907.[108] Shortly after Choong Sup Park moved to Hanford and picked grapes in Fresno.[109] In early 1909, he relocated to Redlands and joined the Industrial Company. Sometime in 1910, Choong Sup Park again moved to Riverside. He also donated $10 to help victims of the Redlands fire.[110] He worked as a labor contractor for the Korean Labor Bureau in Riverside around 1913.[111] When the Great Citrus Freeze of

1913 hit Pachappa Camp, Korean immigrants were struck hard, many were unable to pay the annual duty fund for the Korean independence movement and were faced with economic hardship. Choong Sup Park declared that he would loan duty fund money to members for the greater good of the Korean National Association.[112] Choong Sung Park became a successful farmer and owned a fifteen-acre vegetable farm in Riverside around 1923.[113] In 1927, Choong Sup Park, Sang Sup Park, and Jung Sup Koo jointly opened a big grocery market in Riverside with an initial capital of $1,200. The fruit and vegetable store was located on a busy street and did very well; it raked in a daily income of $70–80 and sometimes up to $100.[114] The store became one of the largest markets in Riverside as the monthly sales volume reached $10,000 in March and April of 1927.[115] Choong Sup Park moved to Los Angeles in 1931 and opened a fruit store on Beverly Blvd in Los Angeles.[116]

Choong Sup Park originally came from Chonju, Cholla Province in South Korea. His wife Jung Kyung Lee arrived in San Francisco in 1915, perhaps as a picture bride.[117] Park and Lee got married in a Korean church in San Francisco on July 28, 1915 and left for Riverside on August 1, 1915. They held a big reception in Riverside.[118] Jung Kyung was hospitalized after giving birth and having appendix complications in 1923.[119] She also actively participated in the independence movement by contributing funds and providing food during meetings. She also served as treasurer of the Korean Patriotic Women's League in 1934. Eventually, the Park family decided to bring their mother Sang Soon Park to Riverside in 1922.[120] Sang Soon Park was sixty years old when she came to Riverside. She passed away in November 1943 and was buried at Rosedale Cemetery in Los Angeles.[121] Young Sup Park was the younger brother of Choong Sup Park and he arrived in America via the *SS China* in 1917. He studied electronics and carpentry in Riverside in 1923 and moved to Los Angeles in 1924.[122] He married Wha Soon Kim on Thanksgiving Day, November 24, 1927, in Los Angeles.[123]

Choong Sup Park and his wife Jung Kyung Park had three sons and one daughter. The eldest son Woon Ha married Yu Hee Han (daughter of Si Dae Han) in March 1943 in Los Angeles.[124] During World War II, all three sons enlisted in the U.S. military and were honorably discharged.[125]

JUNG SUP KOO FAMILY

In the beginning, Jung Sup Koo lived in Green River, California, around 1909 and moved to Riverside in 1912. He was elected to the Aid Affairs board in 1913, the Judicial Affairs board in 1914, and as a Duty Fund representative in 1917 of the Riverside chapter of the Korean National Association. In 1917 and 1918, he was elected as the president of the Riverside chapter of the

Korean National Association.[126] When he was unable to attend his mother's funeral service in Korea, he expressed pain and regret in a *Sinhan Minbo* (August 15, 1918) article. His wife Ae Joo Park arrived in San Francisco via the *S.S. China* in 1917 along with ten other Korean immigrants. Ae Joo Park was already engaged with Jung Sup Park when she came to America.[127] Three picture brides arrived in San Francisco on the *S.S. China*: Kuk Hee Han married Won Sook Song of Woodland; Ae Joo Park married Jung Sup Koo of Riverside; Myung Oak Lee married Hak Bin Suh of Los Angeles. Reverend David Lee served as an officiating pastor of a joint marriage ceremony held at a Korean church in San Francisco.[128] Jung Sup Koo and Ae Joo Park held a reception on May 23 in Riverside.[129]

Ae Joo Park was the sister of Choong Sup and Young Sup Park and was close with her brothers. She became a member of the Korean Patriotic Women's League along with her mother and sister-in-law during the 1940s.[130] Jung Sup Koo and Ae Joo Koo had one son and five daughters. The first son Walter and their eldest daughter Grace were born in Riverside.[131] Florence Koo was born on January 12, 1930, in Alhambra, California. The Koo family owned and operated a fruits and vegetable store in the city at the time.[132] Florence graduated from Santa Ana middle school with honors in 1944.[133] Walter Koo enlisted in the U.S. Army and fought on the Yugoslavia front and became Missing in Action (MIA). However, he was found by a local farmer and rescued.[134]

WOON KYUNG LEE FAMILY

Woon Kyung Lee—Wife

Shumney (Soon Hee) Lee
William Lee
Esther Lee
Addie Lee
Katherine Lee
Kimsie Lee (Mother of Woon Kyung Lee)

Woon Kyung Lee's original name was Won Kil Lee, but he changed it to Woon Kyung to bring luck.[135] According to a 1910 U.S. Census report, Woon Kyung Lee's household included Mrs. W. K. Lee, Shumney Lee, William Lee, Esther Lee, Addie Lee Katherine Lee, and Woon Kyung Lee's mother Kimpsi Lee. In other words, they had one son and four daughters. In 1905, Won Kil (Woon Kyung) Lee resided in San Rafael and contributed $5 to support the *Gongnip Sinbo* newspaper. He must have been fluent in English as he delivered a speech in English during a Korean student meeting in San Francisco in 1906. He moved to Redlands in 1906 and lived there until 1917. He became interim president of the Redlands chapter of the Cooperative Association in 1907. He moved to Riverside in 1918 and became very active in the Riverside chapter of the Korean National Association. Woon Kyung Lee and his wife and mother played major roles in maintaining the declining Korean community in Riverside in 1918 and 1919. Woon Kyung Lee delivered congratulatory remarks during the Korean National Association Foundation Day ceremony in Riverside in 1918.[136] The women of the Lee family also were very active in contributing to the independence fund and attending meetings and rallies, thus keeping the spirit of the movement alive.[137] Woon Kyung Lee's mother, Kimsie Lee, decided to donate all her earnings for the independence of Korea. She was working at a nearby hospital and led a boycott of Japanese soy sauce and products. Kimsie Lee died on January 19, 1926, and was buried at Evergreen Cemetery in Riverside. Her headstone reads, "Woon Kyung Lee's mother" instead of her name Kimsie Lee as many Korean women were silenced and nameless following Confucian values.

In 1923, Woon Kyung Lee owned a grocery store in Los Angeles, but his residence was in Riverside.[138] It appears that Woon Kyung Lee's family continued to reside on Vine Street in Riverside through World War II. According to a *Sinhan Minbo* report, William Lee's parents resided on Vine Street in Riverside in 1943.[139] William Lee served as a second lieutenant in the U.S. Army during World War II. Interestingly, Woon Kyung Lee taught Korean to soldiers at the University of Washington in 1943.[140] Korean immigrants and second generation showed their loyalty and patriotism to both Korea and the United States by enlisting in the U.S. Army, Navy, Air Force, and even teaching the Korean language to soldiers.

In this chapter, I traced the family-tree of several Korean immigrant households at Pachappa Camp in Riverside during the early twentieth century. One of the unique characteristics of Pachappa Camp is that it was a family-based community, unlike other locations that consisted primarily of young bachelors. Women and children were an integral part of the Pachappa Camp community. Birthday party, ceremonies, discussion groups, wedding ceremonies, and other daily activities were held at the camp. The presence of women and children at Pachappa Camp made it a community rather than bachelor labor camp.

NOTES

1. *Sinhan Minbo*, April 29, 1915.
2. *Gongnip Sinbo*, December 6, 1905.
3. *Ibid.*

4. *Gongnip Sinbo*, December 21, 1905.

5. *Gongnip Sinbo*, June 21, 1907.

6. *Gongnip Sinbo*, September 13, 1907.

7. *Sinhan Minbo*, April 7, 1909.

8. *Sinhan Minbo*, March 24, 1909.

9. *Sinhan Minbo*, June 30, 1909.

10. *Sinhan Minbo*, July 7, 1909.

11. *Sinhan Minbo*, August 25, 1909.

12. *Sinhan Minbo*, July 14, 1909.

13. *Sinhan Minbo*, October 5, 1910.

14. *Sinhan Minbo*, November 16, 1910.

15. *Ibid.*

16. *Sinhan Minbo*, June 14, 1911.

17. *Sinhan Minbo*, November 20, 1911.

18. *Sinhan Minbo*, January 29, 1912.

19. *Sinhan Minbo*, December 9, 1912.

20. *Sinhan Minbo*, June 23, 1913.

21. *Sinhan Minbo*, June 17, 1915.

22. *Sinhan Minbo*, October 10, 1918.

23. *Sinhan Minbo*, April 23, 1920.

24. Violet Kim kept this affidavit in her house and gave it to author before she passed away in March 2018.

25. *Sinhan Minbo*, September 27, 1923.

26. *Sinhan Minbo*, April 7, 1921.

27. *Sinhan Minbo*, January 19, 1922.

28. *Sinhan Minbo*, September 27, 1923.

29. *Sinhan Minbo*, May 27, 1926.

30. *Sinhan Minbo*, March 8, 1944.

31. *Sinhan Minbo*, May 23, 1940.

32. *Sinhan Minbo*, December 9, 1912.

33. *Sinhan Minbo*, April 23, 1914.

34. *Sinhan Minbo*, June 21, 1917.

35. *Sinhan Minbo*, June 11, 1925.

36. *Sinhan Minbo*, December 30, 1926.

37. *Gongnip Hyophoe*, May 10, 1907.

38. *Gongnip Hyohoe*, June 14, 1907.

39. *Sinhan Minbo*, February 8, 1916.

40. *Sinhan Minbo*, December 7, 1916.

41. *Sinhan Minbo*, September 6, 1917.

42. *Sinhan Minbo*, January 24, 1918.

43. Interview with Ellen Thun by Edward T. Chang in Riverside on July 1, 1992.

44. Ancestry.com: Honolulu, Hawaii, Passenger and Crew Lists, 1900–1959.

45. Interview with Ellen Thun by Edward T. Chang in Riverside on July 1, 1992.

46. Interview with Ellen Thun by Edward T. Chang on February 23, 1993, at her apartment in Los Angeles.

47. *Ibid.*

48. *Gongnip Sinbo*, December 20, 1907.

49. Interview with Ellen Thun by Edward T. Chang in Riverside on July 1, 1992.

50. Interview with Ellen Thun by Edward T. Chang in Riverside on July 1, 1992.

51. *Sinhan Minbo*, March 7, 1918.

52. *Sinhan Minbo*, October 11, 1919.

53. Interview with Ellen Thun by Edward T. Chang on February 23, 1993, at her apartment in Los Angeles.

54. *Ibid.*

55. Interview with Ellen Thun by Edward T. Chang on February 23, 1993, at her apartment in Los Angeles.

56. *Ibid.*

57. *Ibid.*

58. Ellen Thun, "Heartwarmers" Korea Times. March 1, 1995: 3.

59. Interview with Ellen Thun by Edward T. Chang on February 23, 1993, at her apartment in Los Angeles.

60. *Sinhan Minbo*, July 5, 1934. According to this article, Amos Thun and John Chung were admitted to the California Technical University.

61. *Sinhan Minbo*, October 4, 1945.

62. *Sinhan Minbo*, July 15, 1943.

63. Interview with Ellen Thun by Edward T. Chang on February 23, 1993, at her apartment in Los Angeles.

64. *Ibid.*

65. Ibid.

66. Although Nak Chung Thun and Nak Choon are brothers, they chose to use different spelling for last name.

67. *Sinhan Minbo*, October 13, 1913.

68. Interview with Ellen Thun by Edward T. Chang on February 23, 1993, at her apartment in Los Angeles.

69. Interview with Ellen Thun by Edward T. Chang on February 23, 1993, at her apartment in Los Angeles

70. *Ibid.*

71. *Ibid.*

72. *Ibid.*

73. *Sinhan Minbo*, December 26, 1929.

74. *Sinhan Minbo*, August 25, 1932. "Successful Olympics Games"

75. Interview with Ellen Thun by Edward T. Chang on February 23, 1993, at her apartment in Los Angeles.

76. If you search Kyung Mu (Jacob) Dunn in Korean search website, his birth year is unknown. However, Ellen Thun told me he was born in 1899.

77. *Sinhan Minbo*, October 26, 1910.

78. *Sinhan Minbo*, November 20, 1911.

79. *Sinhan Minbo*, July 12, 1917.

80. *Sinhan Minbo*, March 25, 1919.

81. *Sinhan Minbo*, December 14, 1922.

82. *Sinhan Minbo*, July 10, 1930.

83. *Sinhan Minbo*, March 31, 1932.

84. *Sinhan Minbo*, March 29, 1919.

85. *Sinhan Minbo*, April 6, 1944.

86. K. W. Lee with Luke Kim and Grace Kim, Lonesome Journey collection unpublished manuscript.

87. *Gongnip Sinbo*, November 15, 1907.

88. *Gongnip Sinbo*, December 27, 1907; January 15, 1908.

89. *Sinhan Minbo*, January 12, 1910.

90. *Sinhan Minbo*, May 21, 1914.

91. *Sinhan Minbo*, March 13, 1919.

92. *Sinhan Minbo*, July 1, 1926.

93. *Sinhan Minbo*, October 17, 1929.

94. *Sinhan Minbo*, April 7, 1909.

95. *Sinhan Minbo*, April 14, 1909.

96. *Sinhan Minbo*, July 27, 1910.

97. *Sinhan Minbo*, July 26, 1919.

98. *Sinhan Minbo*, August 3, 1916.

99. *Sinhan Minbo*, October 10, 1918.

100. Edward T. Chang and Woo Sung Han, *Korean American Pioneer Aviators: The Willows Airmen*. Lanham: The Lexington Books, 2015.

101. *Sinhan Minbo*, January 12, 1910.

102. *Sinhan Minbo*, December 25, 1941.

103. *Sinhan Minbo*, June 14, 1945.

104. *Sinhan Minbo*, December 12, 1918, reported that they are planning to get marry on January 1, 1919.

105. *Sinhan Minbo*, June 18, 1942, announced that they are planning to marry on June 21, 1942.

106. *Sinhan Minbo*, August 11, 1938.

107. *Gongnip Sinbo*, May 10, 1907 reported that Choong Sup Park paid $1 to Riverside chapter of Cooperative Association.

108. *Gongnip Sinbo*, June 14, 1907.

109. *Gongnip Sinbo*, August 19, 1908.

110. *Sinhan Minbo*, May 11, 1910.

111. *Sinhan Minbo*, November 28, 1913.

112. *Sinhan Minbo*, April 29, 1915.

113. *Sinhan Minbo*, June 14, 1923.

114. *Sinhan Minbo*, July 19, 1923.

115. *Sinhan Minbo*, August 11, 1927.

116. *Sinhan Minbo*, August 20, 1931, and September 17, 1931.

117. *Sinhan Minbo*, July 22, 1915.

118. *Sinhan Minbo*, August 5, 1915.

119. *Sinhan Minbo*, October 4, 1923.

120. *Sinhan Minbo*, October 19, 1922.

121. *Sinhan Minbo*, November 11, 1943.

122. *Sinhan Minbo*, October 4, 1923.
123. *Sinhan Minbo*, December 1, 1927.
124. *Sinhan Minbo*, March 11, 1943.
125. *Sinhan Minbo*, May 14, 1942.
126. *Sinhan Minbo*, November 29, 1917; December 26, 1918.
127. *Sinhan Minbo*, May 10, 1917.
128. *Sinhan Minbo*, May 17, 1917.
129. *Sinhan Minbo*, June 7, 1917.
130. *Sinhan Minbo*, August 29, 1940.
131. *Sinhan Minbo*, December 26, 1918; January 21, 1921.
132. *Sinhan Minbo*, January 23, 1930.
133. *Sinhan Minbo*, June 8, 1944.
134. *Sinhan Minbo*, October 5, 1944.
135. *Sinhan Minbo*, January 12, 1910.
136. *Sinhan Minbo*, January 24, 1918.
137. Sinhan Minbo, April 19, 1919; June 14, 1919.
138. *Sinhan Minbo*, September 27, 1923.
139. *Sinhan Minbo*, June 10, 1943.
140. *Sinhan Minbo*, October 7, 1943.

Chapter Five

Last Journey to America

The Deportation of Dosan Ahn Chang Ho (1924–1926)

According to Hyung-chan Kim, author of *Tosan Ahn Chang-Ho: A Profile of a Prophetic Patriot*, "Ahn Chang Ho was a towering historic figure who dwarfs in significance most Korean nationalists involved in the development of modern Korean nationalism during the period of Japanese colonial domination over Korea that spanned the five decades between 1895 and 1945."[1] Renowned Korean philosopher and educator Ahn, Pyeong-uk, described Dosan Ahn Chang Ho as a great patriot, educator, philosopher, pioneer, and leader of the Korean independence movement.[2] Dosan Ahn Chang Ho is one of the most respected pioneers and leaders of the early Korean immigrant community in the United States. Comparable to Gandhi of India and Sun Yat-sen of China, Ahn Chang Ho was an ethico-spiritual leader and republican revolutionary. As a revolutionary-democrat, Ahn Chang Ho not only championed constitutional democracy but also led the efforts for in the war for Korea's independence.[3]

Ahn's legacy continues today as many Koreans around the world respect and admire his dedication, sacrifice, and love for his homeland. His efforts and actions in his own life paint a picture of a man true to his word and convictions. He gave his life to transform Korea. During an interrogation by the Japanese police, Ahn declared his fervor for the freedom of Korea: "Yes, I regard the very act of eating an act on behalf of independence and the very act of sleeping an act on behalf of independence. Until this body is destroyed, I will never be any different." More importantly, Ahn Chang Ho was an American pioneer who was influenced by Christianity and pragmatism. His conversion to Christianity made him realize the need to commit to strong personal morality, to the virtue in working for desired objectives, and to the value of service to others. With his newly found pioneer spirit, Dosan organized, educated, and mobilized Korean immigrants in the United States.

He told Korean immigrants to become good citizens and to have a sense of civic responsibility to both America and Korea. Ahn Chang Ho's influence and legacy goes well beyond Korea. He believed and practiced the universal values of honesty, trust, praxis, and bravery. One of his most famous quotes is, "I shall never lie, and only the one with honesty can truly win at the end."[4] He believed that dishonesty was a sin.

Dosan travelled extensively to China, Russia, Europe, Mexico, Australia, Canada, and America—three times—for the Korean independence movement. Ahn Chang Ho first came to America in 1902 with his wife, Hyeryun (Helen) and stayed until early 1907. Dosan returned to America in September 1911 and stayed until 1919. Dosan's third and final trip to America was between 1924 and 1926. The purpose of this paper is to retrace Dosan's final journey to America and investigate why and how he was deported from the United States to Australia in 1926.

As it turns out, Dosan Ahn Chang Ho was interrogated by the U.S. Immigration Service in Chicago on June 3, 1925, on allegations that he was a Bolshevist. Dosan Ahn Chang Ho, the *Heungsadan*, and Korean National Association were accused of being Bolshevist organizations by Kong Wong and Charles Hong Lee who sent a letter to the Immigration Service in 1924. The Immigration Service immediately launched an investigation of Ahn Chang Ho and the organizations he established. Although Ahn Chang Ho was allowed to extend his stay in America for an additional six months despite the investigation, he was eventually deported by the Immigration Service in March 1926. Although Dosan's visa extension request was approved, the Immigration Service did not trust him and decided to deport him. Based on newly discovered Immigration Service documents and *Sinhan Minbo* articles, this paper firmly concludes that Dosan Ahn Chang Ho was deported by the Immigration Service in 1926, and he was never allowed to be reunited with his family in America. Ralph Ahn, the youngest son of Doan Ahn Chang Ho, has never seen his father as Dosan left San Francisco on March 2, 1926, while his wife Helen was pregnant. Years later, Ahn was arrested by the Japanese police in 1932 in Shanghai and died in 1938 due to harsh imprisonment and torture. Dosan Ahn Chang Ho's last journey begins with a letter sent by Kong Wong and Charles Hong Lee accusing him of being a Bolshevist.

DOSAN AHN CHANG HO: BOLSHEVIST?

The Immigration Service in San Francisco received a letter written by Kong Wong and Charles Hong Lee on December 15, 1924.[5] According to the letter, Dosan Ahn Chang Ho was scheduled to arrive in San Francisco the next day, December 16, 1926. The letter was written on Arlington Hotel stationary in

Santa Barbara, California. "Dear Sir—Hereby I enclosed photo of Bolshevist leader your office to look out for him. Understand his coming via Honolulu with few day to your harbor."[6] The letter accuses Dosan Ahn Chang Ho and the *Heungsadan* (Young Korean Academy) as Bolshevists and urged the Immigration Service to send him back to China.[7] On December 24, 1925, the U.S. Department of Labor Immigration Service officially launched an investigation of Ahn Chang Ho.

> You will note that AHN CHANG HO was admitted as a Section 6 traveler under the Exclusion Law and under section 3, Subdivision 2 (alien visiting the United States temporarily as tourist), of the Immigration Act of 1924; that he expressed an intention at the office of America Consul in Shanghai of remaining in the United States for a period approximately eight months and that his object in coming to this country was to visit his wife and children in Los Angeles, their address being given as 106 N. Figueroa St., your city. Subsequent to the admission of the applicant we received the letter which you will find enclosed from one Kong Wong, alias Charles Hong Lee (or possibly these two names represent two different persons), written in Santa Barbara, Cal., the date of which is not given but which letter was received here on December 15, too late to be given consideration in the disposition of this case. The information given in the letter may or may not be authentic, but it would seem as the same should be given attention in the hearing conducted in your district.[8]

Since this letter was received one day before Dosan arrived in San Francisco, the Immigration Service was unable to process it in a timely manner. However, this document makes clear that the investigation was launched because of the letter sent by Kong Wong and/or Charles Hong Lee. It also raises questions about the purpose of his visit to the United States. In his application, Ahn Chang Ho expressed the purpose of his visit was to see his wife and children in Los Angeles. But when Dosan Ahn Chang Ho traveled extensively throughout the United States, it raised the suspicion of the Immigration Service Inspector because it seemed the purpose of his visit to the United States was different from what he initially stated.

The Immigration Service tried to locate Dosan Ahn Chang Ho, however, he travelled to the East extensively during this time and they were unable to track him down. An Immigration Service Chicago office report dated April 28, 1925 noted that Ahn Chang Ho was travelling to the East and was scheduled to return within thirty days.[9] On May 8, 1925, the Immigration Service in San Francisco sent a notice to the Los Angeles office to assist them in locating Dosan Ahn Chang Ho and to let them know immediately of any new information.[10] The Immigration Service Office District Director in Los Angeles made an effort to locate the writer(s)—Kong Wong and/or Charles Hong Lee—of the Santa Barbara letter, but no information was found.[11] I also tried to search for the identity of Charles Hong Lee, but could not locate him. I was able to locate the name Chai Hong Lee who came to the United States as a foreign student in 1923 to attend Hastings College. However, I could not positively identify Chai Hong Lee as Charles Hong Lee.[12]

On June 3, 1925, Dosan Ahn Chang Ho was interrogated by Immigrant Inspector J. B. Brekke at the Chicago Immigration Service office.[13] "Are you interested in the Soviet Government of Russia?" Brekke asked Dosan who answered no. The inspector also asked if Ahn, "advocated radical changes in the Government of the United States?" Ahn answered, "never." Three days later, on June 6, the Immigration Service Chicago Office sent three copies of statements made by Ahn Chang Ho to the Los Angeles Office.[14] On June 9, 1925, the Immigration Service Los Angeles Office returned all relevant documents back to the San Francisco Office under the subject: "AHN CHANG HO, Korean, under investigation: Your file No. 23880/1-6 is herewith returned."[15] It officially confirmed that Ahn Chang Ho was being investigated as a Bolshevist. Despite the investigation, Dosan applied for a temporary extension visa so he could stay in the United States a little longer. "To date it has not been possible to confirm the allegations set forth in said letter, but we feel that the Bureau should have before it all information available when passing on the pending application."[16] Finally, Ahn Chang Ho's temporary stay extension application was approved by the Bureau of Immigration, Washington on July 11, 1925.[17] The Immigration Service San Francisco Office sent the official approval letter to Ahn Chang Ho's 106 North Figueroa address on July 22, 1925. The letter stated that "your temporary admission has been extended for a period of six months from Aug. 16, 1925. Please be guided accordingly."[18] Ahn Chang Ho sent a "thank you" letter on Young Korean Academy stationary to the Immigration Service San Francisco Office on August 6, 1925. "I wish to express my sincere appreciation for your kind and prompt consideration of it. It [is] nevertheless my regret that your letter could not reach me any sooner on account of my trip to the East. Consequently, I am in delay of extending these few lines of appreciation."

Hyung-chan Kim also wrote about the Bolshevist investigation by the U.S. Immigration Service Office on the *Heungsadan* (Young Korean Academy). However, he did not know why and how the investigation was launched. "In the absence of any document it is difficult to ascertain who or what was responsible for informing the U.S. immigration authorities of the *Heungsadan* activities."[19] We do know for sure that the letter sent by Kong Wong and/or Charles Hong Lee triggered an official investigation. The Immigration Service tried to locate the identity of Kong Wong and/or Charles Hong Lee, but was unsuccessful. I also tried to identify Kong Wong and/or Charles Hong Lee, but I could not find him. It is also noteworthy that the letter not only accused Ahn Chang Ho of being a Bolshevist but also the *Heungsadan* and the Korean National Association. I can only assume that Kong Wong and/or Charles Hong Lee was/were supporters of Syngman Rhee who established the *Dongjihoe* (Comrade Association) in 1921. The Comrade Association and the Korean National Association were competing for members and organizational influence throughout the United States at the time. It is logical to assume that the Comrade Association tried to block the return of Dosan Ahn Chang Ho to the United States to limit the influence of the Korean National Association and the Young Korean Academy. Others also have noted the false socialist and communist accusations against Dosan Ahn Chang Ho. Hyung-Chan Kim also mentioned a conversation between Kwak Nim-tae and Philip Jaisohn that documented the false allegations Dosan was accused of.

> According to Jaisohn, Tosan had been denied a U.S. visa to return to the United States in 1924, because a Korean leader stationed in Washington, DC had accused Tosan of being a Communist. Kwak asked Jaisohn who such a person could be, and Jaisohn responded to him almost in anger, "You mean you don't know who that leader is?" Kwak thought that Jaisohn implicated Syngman Rhee.[20]

Kim also cited another source to corroborate this story. "According to Kim Hyeon-gu, Syngman Rhee reported to the U.S. intelligence authorities that Ahn Chang-ho, Pak Yong-man and Kimm Kiusic were radical communists. Syngman Rhee claimed that he did so out of his loyalty to America where he was allowed to live and that he was proud of what he had done."[21] If this story is accurate, Syngman Rhee did not hesitate to accuse leaders that opposed him, people like Ahn Chang Ho, Pak Yong-man and Kimm Kiusic, as communists. It is almost certain that Kong Wong and/or Charles Hong Lee is (were) followers of Syngman Rhee or perhaps he/they were actually Syngman Rhee himself. Also, some confusion regarding the timing of Dosan's arrest and eventual deportation must be clarified. "It was claimed by Kim San that Tosan was arrested in 1924 for communist books he kept in his Los Angeles home,[22] and in Tosan's letter of June 24, 1925, he told his wife that he was investigated by U.S. authorities who came to visit with him at [the] Heungsadan headquarters office, because someone had informed them that Tosan was a communist."[23]

Since an official investigation of Dosan Ahn Chang Ho began on December 24, 1924, it is highly unlikely that Dosan was arrested for possession of communist books in 1924. According to Immigration Service Office documents, investigators began looking for Dosan Ahn Chang Ho in the spring of 1925. They visited the *Heungsadan* building at 106 North Figueroa Street in Los Angeles to investigate, but they were unable to locate him because Dosan had travelled to the East. Finally, the Immigration Service Office tracked him down and interrogated him on June 3, 1925, at their Chicago office. It is also noteworthy to correct that Dosan was not denied a visa to enter the United States in 1924 as claimed by Philip Jaisohn, instead he was allowed to enter but was later forced to leave the United States in March 1926.

While visiting Chicago, Ahn Chang Ho continued to meet with students and Korean immigrants in mid-west communities. For example, the *Sinhan Minbo* (July 16, 1925) reported that "according to a Korean student at Chicago University, Dosan Ahn Chang Ho travelled to several places and was planning to depart Chicago on the eighth to visit Detroit, Cleveland, South Bend, and Kansas City." Ahn Chang Ho was forced to stop his planned trip to the East and returned to San Francisco in late July 1925. The *Sinhan Minbo* (July 30, 1925) reported on Dosan's travels and his circumstance.

After visiting several Korean communities in the East, Dosan Ahn Chang Ho safely returned to San Francisco. Initially, Ahn planned to visit as many places as possible, however, he regrets that he was forced to stop and return to the West for two reasons: (1) he had not secured temporary stay extension permission from the State Department, (2) he ran out of funding, thus, he was unable to continue to travel East. Ahn expressed deep regret for not visiting several places to meet with students and immigrants." Ahn expressed his regret in a letter he sent to the Immigration Service dated August 6, 1925 that "It is nevertheless my regret that your letter could not reach me any sooner on account of my trip to the East.[24]

In the meantime, the Immigration Service continued its own investigation of Ahn Chang Ho. The Director of the Immigration Office in Chicago, Howard D. Ebey, sent the entire Ahn Chang Ho investigation files to the Los Angeles District Director of Immigration dated June 6, 1925. "Referring to your letter of April 23, 1925, No. 25140/24. Relating to AHN CHANG HO, I am returning herewith San Francisco file No. 23880/1-6 and enclose three copies of statement made by Ahn Chang Ho at this office."[25] Three days later on June 9, 1925, the Assistant district Director of the office of the District Director in Los Angeles, Calif., sent all the files to the Commissioner of Immigration in San Francisco under the subject heading "AHN CHANG HO, Korean, under investigation." It reads as follows: "Referring to your communication of the 8th ultimo, there is herewith enclosed, in duplicate, transcript of the examination of this alien conducted by Inspector Brekke at Chicago, Illinos, on the 3rd instant. Your file No. 23880/1-6 is herewith returned." It means that they finished their official investigation of Ahn Chang Ho and were waiting on a final decision. On June 24, 1925, the U.S. Department of Labor Immigration Service filled out Ahn Chang Ho's "Certificate of

Admission of Alien" form. "I hereby certify that the following is a correct record and statement of facts relative to the admission to the United States of the alien named below." The certificate included basic information on Ahn Chang Ho's date of arrival, vassal name, age, occupation, marital status etc. Interestingly Ahn's race is recorded as Chinese. Since Ahn arrived with a Chinese passport, perhaps Ahn was a Chinese legally.

On June 26, 1925, the Immigration Service District No. 30, Office of the Commissioner Angel Island Station via Ferry Post Office San Francisco wrote a general letter on the current state of the investigation of Ahn Chang Ho.

> The applicant's travel in the United States has been extensive, the purpose there-fore as claimed by him entirely different from that alleged in letter signed Kong Wong and Charles Long Lee, without date, received at this office on Dec. 15, 1924, or several days after the alien was admitted. To date it has not been pos-sible to confirm the allegations set forth in said letter, but we feel that the Bureau should have before it all information available when passing on the pending application. The file attached should be returned after it has served its purpose.[26]

This document suggests that the allegations against Ahn Chang Ho by Kong Wong and/or Charles Hong Lee could not be verified nor credible. Finally, the Bureau of Immigration Washington issued a visa extension ap-proval letter dated July 11, 1925. "With reference to your letter the 26th ultimo, No. 12025/02, you are advised that the Department has directed the temporary admission of Ahn Chang Ho be extended for a period of six months from the date of expiration of the eight months which have heretofore been granted him. The file forwarded by your office is returned herewith."[27] Therefore, Ahn Chang Ho could stay in the United States until February 16, 1926, since he was officially admitted on December 16, 1924.

After receiving the temporary stay extension letter from the Immigration Service Office, Ahn continued to visit and meet with students and immi-grants, however, he mostly stayed in California between August of 1925 and March of 1926.[28] The *Sinhan Minbo* (November 12, 1925) reported that "Dosan Ahn Chang Ho is visiting Dinuba and Taft (California) and will arrive in San Francisco soon." According to Hyung-chan Kim, Ahn Chang Ho was refused service at a hot springs when he was visiting Stockton, Taft, and Chico.[29] In California, anti-Asian sentiment was still very high and Asian immigrants often faced overt racial discrimination. It was very common for restaurants not to serve Asian American customers—signs of-ten read "No Dog or Chinese Allowed." Dosan Ahn Chang Ho visited Taft again in February 1926 after he left San Francisco on a Saturday; he was scheduled to return home later.[30]

DEPORTATION

By early 1926, Ahn was preparing to return to China as his visa extension was expiring. He initially planned to visit the Korean community in Hawaii for two weeks before returning to China. It appears that the Immigration Service Office was unsure if Ahn Chang Ho was a Bolshevist despite the fact that they couldn't corroborate the accusations against him. What was clear, however, was that the Immigration Service Office was determined to deport Ahn Chang Ho because his extension visa expired. The Immigration Service Office of the Commissioner Angel Island Station prepared a document to ensure Ahn Chang Ho's departure from the United States.

> There are attached all papers relating to the alien AHN CHANG HO, in order that you may arrange to have his sailing for Australia witnessed. As he stated, verbally, that he would leave for February 23 or 24 by S.S. "Sonoma" by Union Steamship Company, it is uncertain whether he meant by S.S. "Sonoma" February 23, 1926, Oceanic Steamship Co. or S.S. "Makura," Feb. 24, 1926, Union Steamship co.[31]

In February 23, 1926, the Immigration Office at Angel Island certified that Ahn Chang Ho boarded the S.S. Sonoma and departed from San Francisco. "I hereby certify that I this day checked out on the S.S. Sonoma, a certain Chinese named "AHN CHANG HO" and identified him by his photograph on his certificate which with file is hereto enclosed."[32] However, the same document shows that Ahn Chang Ho "checked out on the S.S. Sonoma on March 2, 1926, and that the vessel had originally sailed from the San Francisco port on February 23, 1926, but returned for repairs, thus delaying Ahn's departure." According to Hyung-chan Kim, "In San Pedro, near Los Angeles, Tosan went aboard the S.S. Sonoma that carried him toward, Hawaii, but it developed propeller trouble during the voyage and was forced to return to San Francisco for repair."[33] Obviously, Ahn Chang Ho did not depart from San Pedro as described by Hyung-chan Kim. The *Sinhan Minbo* (February 25, 1926) reported the story of Ahn's departure in an article titled "Ahn Dosan Farewell Party." The story also corroborates the Immigration Office document which states he left from San Francisco. According to the *Sinhan Minbo article,* "Ahn's Farewell Party was held at a Korean church in San Francisco on the evening of the 22nd." Ahn urged fellow Korean Americans to do their best to achieve independence of Korea. In addition, he thanked everyone who attended his farewell party in Los Angeles, San Francisco, and Stockton. According to Ahn's boarding record dated March 2, 1926, Ahn received permission to board on February 20, 1926, in San Francisco. Therefore, we can safely conclude that Ahn boarded the S.S. Sonoma on February 23, 1926, from San Francisco and that the ship was forced to return to San Francisco because of a propeller malfunction. The S.S. Sonoma was repaired and departed from San Francisco on March 2, 1926.

Mrs. Ahn initially wanted to come to San Francisco to send her husband off to China on February 23, 1926. However, Dosan Ahn Chang Ho urged her to stay home and she did not travel to San Francisco. However, when she heard the news that the S.S. Sonoma had returned to San Francisco for ship repair, she decided to go to San Francisco on March 2 to send him off. According to the *Sinhan Minbo* (March 4, 1926), she told her husband "Pyonganhi Gasipsi Yo, Pyonganhi Gasipsi Yo" (Please be safe, please be safe) as the S.S. Sonoma began sailing from the port of San Francisco. It was the final good-bye for the couple who had endured so much as Dosan Ahn Chang Ho never returned to the United States to see his wife and children. The S.S. Sonoma arrived in Honolulu, Hawaii on March 8, 1926. Dosan Ahn Chang Ho planned to stay in Hawaii for two weeks to meet with Korean American community members and depart for China. However, he was not allowed to stay in Hawaii and was forced to depart for Australia. According to Hyung-chan Kim, Dosan never planned to go to Australia but the "Immigration Office told Dosan that he will not be allowed to stay in Hawaii because Young Korean Academy is a bad organization." Hyung-chan Kim noted that he did not know why the Immigration Service Office told Dosan this due to lack of documentation.[34] We know for sure that the accusation letter sent by Kong Wong and/or Charles Hong Lee opened an investigation of Dosan Ahn Chang Ho and the Young Korean Academy. The *Sinhan Minbo* (March 25, 1925) also reported on what happened to Dosan when he landed in Hawaii.

Dosan Ahn Chang Ho arrived in Honolulu, Hawaii on the 8th around 4 p.m. and the Korean American community planned a welcome party. Initially, Dosan Ahn Chang Ho wanted to stay in Hawaii for two weeks, but the Immigration Office did not allow it and he was forced to leave that same evening. Dosan Ahn Chang Ho stayed in Honolulu, Hawaii only for 6 hours and briefly gave a speech to about 150 Koreans who hastily attended his farewell party. Around 10 p.m. Dosan Ahn Chang Ho left Honolulu, Hawaii.

According to the S.S. Sonoma boarding record, Dosan "continued [his] journey on [the] Sonoma to Australia."[35] It clearly shows that the Immigration Service wanted to make sure to send Dosan Ahn Chang Ho off to Australia on the S.S. Sonoma as the investigation on him was inconclusive. The Immigration Service was unable to verify the "Bolshevist" allegation against Dosan Ahn Chang Ho and they chose to be "safe" by deporting him to Australia.

Dosan Ahn Chang Ho arrived in Australia on March 25, 1926. Dosan felt warmth and less discrimination from the Australian officials compared with the Immigration bureaucrats in the United States. Australian officials allowed him to land without strict enforcement of law.[36] Dosan planned to depart on (April) 14th and arrive in China around the 26th.[37] It is uncertain when Dosan Ahn Chang Ho arrived in Shanghai, but it appears he arrived around May 22, 1926. According to a *Sinhan Minbo* report (June 25, 1926), "Welcoming ceremony was held on May 22, 1926 as the Korean community in Shanghai was glad to welcome Dosan Ahn Chang Ho. Dosan spent two weeks in Shanghai to take care of issues relating to the [Korean] Provisional Government." When Dosan arrived in Shanghai, the Korean Provisional Government was in organizational disarray due to a number of events that had transpired since his departure from China in November 1924.[38] His arrival brought a sense of structure to the provisional government.

Dosan Ahn Chang Ho held an optimistic view of the development of a model community project and began searching for an ideal site. He travelled to Nanjing, Beijing, Manchuria, and even the Philippines in search of an ideal site for his model community project. Dosan determined that Manchuria was not a suitable place for his model community project as he and several Korean leaders were detained by the Chinese police in 1927. In 1929, Dosan decided to visit the Philippines to check out the feasibility of developing his model community project there.[39] Dosan stayed in the Philippines around fifty days and decided to return to China as he did not want to pose a financial burden on the Korean residents in the Philippines. Dosan eventually abandoned the idea of bringing Korean immigrants to the Philippines when the Chief of the Immigration Department of Philippines told Dosan that Korean immigrants would be accepted only if they came on Japanese passports.[40] Dosan planned to bring Korean immigrants on Chinese passports.

Dosan planned to return to the United States to be with his family sometime in 1932. However, he was arrested by French and Japanese police in connection with the bombing incident in Hungkou Park, Shanghai, China by Yun Pong-gil on April 29, 1932. Although Dosan was not connected to the bombing, he was turned over to the Japanese authorities and sent to Incheon, Korea.[41] Dosan was found guilty as charged and sentenced to four years in prison. However, he was released on February 10, 1935, because he was considered a model prisoner. Dosan was imprisoned again on June 28, 1937, and had to endure physical and psychological torture during Japanese police interrogation. When Japanese police asked if he would continue to get involved in Korea's independence movement if he was released, Dosan responded, "Yes, I consider eating an act for independence and sleeping also an act for independence. As long as I live, there will be no change in this."[42] Dosan became gravely ill and was allowed to be released on bail on December 24, 1937. He was immediately hospitalized but died at the hospital on March 10, 1938.

CONCLUSION

Dosan Ahn Chang Ho and the *Heungsadan* were accused of being Bolshevists and a socialist organization by Kong Wong and/or Charles Hong Lee. The events that the accusation set in motion changed the course of Dosan Ahn Chang Ho's life. His wife Helen would never see him again and Dosan would live out the rest of his life away from his family. Although I tried hard to search for the identity of Kong Wong and/or Charles Hong Lee, I could not find any information on the identity of the person who sent the accusatory letter to the Immigration Service Office which launched an extensive investigation and also tried to find the person who sent the letter; they were unsuccessful. Although the Immigration Service Office approved Ahn's extension request to stay in America for an additional six months, a cloud of suspicion overshadowed Dosan. The Immigration Service Office's inconclusive findings regarding Dosan's case did not fall in his favor. The Immigration Service Office decided to deport Dosan Ahn Chang Ho due to the uncertainty. Sadly, Dosan Ahn Chang Ho's youngest son, Ralph Ahn, never saw his father as Dosan never returned to America to be with his family.

In this paper, I tried to retrace why, how, and for what reasons Dosan Ahn Chang Ho was deported on March 2, 1926. The Immigration Service Office conducted an extensive investigation on Dosan Ahn Chang Ho and the *Heungsadan* after it received an accusatory letter from presumably a pro-Syngman Rhee person identifying as Kong Wong and/or Charles Hong Lee. It is possible to assume that a pro-Syngman Rhee group is responsible for the deportation of Dosan Ahn Chang Ho in 1926. Although Dosan Ahn Chang Ho was far from being a Bolshevist or a communist, he faced investigation and eventual deportation based on false allegations from an unknown accuser who was likely a Syngman Rhee supporter. Dosan Ahn Chang Ho was a Christian, educator, and believer of democratic ideals. The deportation and investigation conducted against him were based on nothing, but a letter written by someone whom no one could find.

NOTES

1. Hyung-Chan Kim, *Tosan Ahn Chang-Ho: A Profile of a Prophetic Patriot.* Tosan Memorial Foundation, Seoul. 1996: xv (preface).

2. *Ibid*, Forward.

3. Jacqueline Pak, Ph.D. thesis: School of Oriental and African Studies, University of London, 1999.

4. Korean Independence Hall, installation date, May 13, 1986.

5. Despite *Weekly Chosun* (September 15. 2002. Vol. 1719), reported discovery of immigration file on Dosan Ahn Chang Ho. However, it was not known to author or most people in Korea. Yonhap News and other Korean media wrongly reported that I discovered immigration file on Dosan Ahn Chang Ho.

6. U.S. Department of Labor District No. 30, Immigration Service, Office of the Commissioner Angel Island Station Via Ferry Post Office, December 24, 1924.

7. See appendix 1.

8. U.S. Department of Labor, Immigration Service, Office of the Commissioner Angel Island Station Via Ferry Post Office, December 24, 1924. Document No. 238880/1-6. Investigation Arrival Case Files, San Francisco, Records of the U.S. Immigration and Naturalization Service, RG 85, National Archives, Pacific Region, San Bruno, Ca. All Immigration Service documents in this paper are referred to this reference.

9. U.S. Department of Labor, Immigration Service, Office of Inspector in Chicago, Ill. April 28, 1925. Document No. 2008/967.

10. U.S. Department of Labor, Immigration Service, Office of the Commissioner Angel Island Station Via Ferry Post Office, May 8, 1925. Document No. 238880/1-6.

11. U.S. Department of Labor, Immigration Service, Office of District Director Los Angeles, Calif. May 11, 1925. Document No. 25140/24.

12. Neither Chai Hong Lee's transcript (attached) nor Hastings College yearbooks indicate he graduated. In yearbooks, he is always listed as a special student. For the '23/'24, '24/'25, and '25/'26 academic years, he was an active member of Eta Phi Lambda, a local organization similar to a Greek fraternity without houses. At the time, Dr. Hayes Fuhr, Chair of the Hastings College Music Conservatory, and Dr. Frank Weyer, Dean of the College, served as advisors. The other special student from Korea was Wang Sun Yun. Unfortunately, he died in 1926 of what a later account lists as pneumonia. His father, Tchi O Yun, was the former minister of education in Korea, and his mother was of royal extraction. Accounts note that he was very well-liked and respected on campus and in the community of Hastings. Mr. Yun is buried in Hastings' Parkview Cemetery. A 1937, newspaper account indicates Mr. Yun's brother, Dr. Ilsun S. Yun, visited the grave site. Dr. Yun is noted a "Professor of Pathology at a Korean university."

13. See Appendix 2.

14. U.S. Department of Labor, Immigration Service, Office of Inspector in Chicago, Ill. June 6, 1925. Document No. 2008/967.

15. U.S. Department of Labor, Immigration Service, Office of District Director Los Angeles, Calif. June 9, 1925. Document No. 2008/967.

16. U.S. Department of Labor, Immigration Service, Office of the Commissioner Angel Island Station Via Ferry Post Office, June 26, 1925. Document No. 12025/02

17. U.S. Department of Labor, Bureau of Immigration, Washington. July 11, 1925. Document No. 55466/466.

18. U.S. Department of Labor, Immigration Service, Office of the Commissioner Angel Island Station Via Ferry Post Office July 22, 1925. Document No. 23880/1-6.

19. Hyung-Chan Kim, *Tosan Ahn Chang-Ho: A Profile of a Prophetic Patriot.* Seoul: Korea, Tosan Memorial Foundation, 1996: 225.

20. *Ibid*, 212. Kim cited Yun Pyeong-seok and Yun Kyeong-no, Op.cit, 140–1.

21. Ibid, see footnote 21 in chapter 8. See Ko Cheong-hyu, "Tongnipundonggi Yi Seung-man (Syngman Rhee) eui woekyo noseonkwa chegukjueui (Syngman Rhee's Diplomacy during the Period of the Indendepence Movement and Imperialism)" *Yeoksa Pipyeong* (Critique of History), Winter 1995, No. 31, p.169.

22. Nym Wales and Kim San, Song of Ariran: A Korean Communist in the Chinese Revolution. San Francisco: Ramparts Press, Inc., 1941: 120. Quoted from Hyun-Chan Kim, 1996: 225.

23. Hyung-Chan Kim, 1996: 225.

24. Thank you letter sent by Ahn Chang Ho to Immigration Service San Francisco, August 6, 1925.

25. U.S. Department of Labor Immigration Service Office of District Director Chicago, ILL. June 16, 1925. Document No. 2008/967.

26. U.S. Department of Labor Immigration Service District No. 30, in answering refer to No. 12025/02, June 25, 1925.

27. U.S. Department of Labor Bureau of Immigration Washington document No. 55466/466, July 11, 1925.

28. Kim, 1996: 214.

29. Ibid, 1996: 215. Cited from Tosan's letter to Helen on November 16, 1925.

30. *Sinhan Minbo*, February 11, 1926.

31. U.S. Department of Labor, Immigration Service, Office of the Commissioner Angel Island Station Via Ferry Post Office February 6, 1926. Document No.12025/14120.

32. U.S. Department of Labor, Immigration Service, Office of the Commissioner Angel Island Station Via Ferry Post Office February 23, 1926. Document No. 12025/14120.

33. Kim, 1996: 215–225.

34. Hyung-Chan Kim, 1996:225.

35. S.S. Sonoma boarding record March 2, 1926. Immigration Office file no. 4387/263.

36. *Sinhan Minbo*, April 29, 1926.

37. Ibid.

38. Hyung-chan Kim, 1996: 226.

39. *Sinhan Minbo*, February 21, 1929; May 16, 1929; May 23, 1929.

40. Hyung-chan Kim, 1996: 236.

41. According to *Sinhan Minbo* June 30, 1932, Dosan departed from Shanghai on May 30 and will arrive in Incheon port on June 7.

42. Hyung-chan Kim, 1996: 267. Quoted from Yi Kwang-su, Tosan Ahn Chang Ho ssi eui hwaltong (Tosan Ahn Chang Ho and his Work). Samcheolli, Vol. July 7, 1930: 6–9.

Chapter Six

Point of Cultural Interest
and Dosan Statue

On March 23, 2017, the City of Riverside, California, held an official plaque ceremony to designate the location of Pachappa Camp as its No. 1 "City Point of Cultural Interest." The designation took almost two years to complete with the original application being submitted in February 2015 and a revised version submitted in May 2016.[1] The process involved several checks and balances by the city who used outside historian consultation to confirm our research findings and several meetings. The city's team determined that the site located at 3096 Cottage Street—formerly 1532 Pachappa Avenue—on Assessor Parcel numbers 219-321-001; 219-321-002; and 211-241-011, were of historic value and should be recognized.[2] The 3.5 acre site is owned and occupied by the Southern California Gas Co. and houses its Riverside compressed natural gas base.

The City of Riverside's Historic Preservation officers worked closely with my team and I to ensure our information was accurate by offering feedback,[3] asking questions, and doing their own interest. We had several meetings with the city's staff and mayor who all agreed with our findings and encouraged our application be submitted to City Council for approval. At the same time, Southern California Gas Co. management[4] agreed to allow for their property at the corner of Cottage Street and Commerce Street to be recorded as the city's first Point of Cultural of Interest.

On December 6, 2016, Riverside City Council unanimously approved the designation of the site as its first Cultural Point of Interest. The site, as noted by city council members was clearly the first organized Korean settlement in the United States. The historic site also met two of the evaluation and recognition criteria set forth in the Riverside Municipal Code Section 20.50.010(BB): "Criterion (1) Has anthropological, cultural, military, political, architectural, economic, scientific or technical, religious, experimental, or other value; Criterion (2) The original physical feature(s) no longer exist to an appreciable extent."[5]

Ralph Ahn, Dosan's youngest son attended the meeting and affirmed his support for the recognition and designation of the site by the city. He also reaffirmed that Pachappa was the first organized-Korean American settlement. Speakers and organizations in support of the recognition included the Save Our Chinatown Committee, the Consul General of Korea, Los Angeles office, the Dosan Ahn Chang Ho Memorial Foundation, a student, and more. After all the speakers, questions, and presentations concluded, the council approved the application unanimously.

While the achievement was a milestone for the Korean American community, the road to the recognition was not without some difficulty. Unsupported opposition from Phillip "Flip" Ahn Cuddy, the grandson of Dosan Ahn Chang Ho and the son of Susan Ahn Cuddy was raised through letters, emails, and a meeting.[6] He unsuccessfully attempted to block the designation of Pachappa Camp as the City of Riverside's first Point of Cultural Interest in December 2016. Flip's posts on Facebook and online claim that San Francisco was the first Koreatown.[7] To date, there is no evidence showing that an organized Korean American settlement existed anywhere else until Pachappa Camp was founded by Dosan Ahn Chang Ho in 1905 (possibly late 1904). The city's staff and historian consultant investigated his claims and found no support. In an email dated April 10, 2017, city officials once again reiterated that their findings corroborated our research and that Pachappa Camp should be recognized as the first organized Korean American settlement. City officials responded to Flip's concerns and documented their interactions with him. In an email dated November 1, 2016, the city informed Flip that the interpretation of the historic facts and information by myself and my team, although different from his, "appears to be supported by the recognition application and further strengthened by the additional research and support compiled since the [Cultural Heritage Board] meeting."[8]

Pachappa Camp is now recognized as America's first Koreatown and the site is marked with a sign. The signage was installed at the corner of Cottage and Commerce Streets on December 12, 2017, with the following inscription in English and Korean:

Pachappa Camp was the site of the First Organized Korean American Settlement founded by Dosan Ahn Chang Ho in 1905 at 1532 Pachappa Avenue, now 3096 Cottage Street. Dosan was Korea's most patriotic and dedicated reformer and pioneer known for his role in the Korean Independence Movement. Also known as Dosan's Republic, about one hundred men, women, and children nurtured a community here through activities such as weddings, baptisms, births, English classes, and church services. Pachappa Camp, which included 20-farmed dwellings and a large community center that supported a Korean Labor Bureau, flourished until 1918. By 1920, only a handful of Korean families remained in Riverside.

On March 23, 2017, the Southern California Gas Co. and the YOK Center at UC Riverside honored Pachappa Camp as the first Cultural Point of Interest in the City of Riverside. Attendees included Ralph Ahn, So. Cal. Gas leaders, Korean American community members, and more. The celebration recognized the groundbreaking connection between Riverside and Korean American history.

It's important to note that, Dosan's Republic reveals the importance of place-based memories. By the 1940s, the actual Korean pioneers had disappeared from Riverside. The 1920 Census recorded only four Korean families living in Riverside, none of whom occupied homes along Pachappa Avenue (renamed Commerce Street in 1954) or adjacent Cottage Street.[9] City directories from the mid-1920s listed the sites formerly occupied by the Korean community as either vacant or inhabited by individuals of Japanese or Mexican descent.[10] Hence, people's migration also played a role in diminishing the Korean population and abandoning the landscape as a record of this community's history. Several gravestones of Koreans who lived in Riverside and at Pachappa Camp can be found in at Olivewood Cemetery and Evergreen Cemetery. Soon Hak Kim and his son are among the buried as well as Yong Ryon Kim and Hazel Han Kim.

In the 1950s, crews bulldozed the former Koreatown site to redevelop the land for commercial use. The succeeding oil and gas companies' occupation of the block physically erased the camp's traces from the city's landscape. Visitors to the site today see only parking lots, cinderblock buildings, fueling stations, and fencing. The only vestige of the past remains the adjacent railroad tracks. Due to development and the physical erasure of Pachappa Camp's built environment, Riverside lost sight of its historic Korean community. For years after the camp's demolition, an insurance map of Riverside, city directories, and a rare newspaper article remained the only written sources about Riverside's Koreatown in the English language, limiting the larger public's knowledge about the significance of the site. In 1961, former resident of Dosan's Republic Easurk Emsen Charr published his autobiography, and three decades later, Mary Paik Lee produced her memoir, reflecting on their time spent at Pachappa Camp in the early 1900s.

In the 1990s, the Korean American Museum Oral History Project in Los Angeles also sought to collect testimony from individuals who had lived at the site, such as Helen Lee Hong while John Cha likewise conducted oral histories with past residents. This scholarship has remained instrumental in increasing awareness about Pachappa Camp among second generation Korean Americans and the general public. Nevertheless, none of these works tied the stories of Dosan's Republic back to the physical space where the events occurred: the city of Riverside.

Erecting the statue of Ahn Chang Ho in downtown Riverside in 2001, reestablished a connection between this trailblazing and history-making community and the location where these events transpired. Humans have a strong capacity to create place memories, which scholar Dolores Hayden describes as the "ability to connect with both the built and natural environments that are entwined in cultural landscape."[11] Physical places may act as sites of consciousness, culture, and stories, and they have the power to remind individuals of the past. Erecting Dosan's statue now serves the purpose of reminding the general public about Ahn's time in Riverside and the settlement he grew there. The dedication of the memorial succeeded in reviving interest in the study of Riverside's Koreatown. Korean delegates visiting from Asia showed great interest in seeing the site where Ahn Chang Ho once resided after viewing the memorial, hoping that to know where he lived would bring them closer to the man.[12]

EPILOGUE

Research findings on Pachappa Camp and Dosan Ahn Chang Ho fill a void in Korean American, independence movement, and modern Korean history. Dosan Ahn Chang Ho's biography mentions that he stayed in Riverside as a footnote. The Dosan Memorial Foundation and the *Heungsadan* do not even mention anything about Riverside. And yet, Pachappa Camp should be recognized as one of the most significant historical sites of the early Korean American community for several reasons: (1) Pachappa Camp was the first and largest Koreatown in the United States during the early twentieth century, (2) The *Gongnip Hyophoe* and Dosan Ahn Chang Ho established plans to relocate Korean immigrants who landed in San Francisco to Riverside, (3) Although the headquarters of the *Gongnip Hyophoe* was established in San Francisco, residents of Pachappa Camp played a key role and provided financial and other support, (4) The *Sinminhoe* was initiated in Riverside in 1906, and Dosan Ahn Chang Ho left for Korea in 1907 to engage in secret independence activities, (5) The Korean National Association of North America convention was held in Riverside in 1911, (6) Unlike other Korean immigrant communities elsewhere, Pachappa Camp was a family-based community with women and children, (7) Pachappa camp functioned as base camp for the early Korean immigrant community and as a mecca of the Korean independence movement during the early 1900s, (8) Pachappa Camp was not a typical labor camp because Korean immigrants established a Korean mission and *Hakyo* (Korean school), as well as other cultural activities. They also celebrated birthdays and held wedding ceremonies, public lectures, and established a discussion group. Pachappa Camp was also organized and run by Dosan's principles which included a dress code, curfews, and the community's own policing system. Thus, the evidence is clear, Pachappa Camp was the first organized-Korean American settlement in the United States.

Dosan Ahn Chang Ho was a man of his word who acted upon his words. He was a leader who tried to carry out individual, societal, and national reform at the same time. Dosan established the *Heungsadan* (Young Korean Academy) to change and/or reform individuals.

> The purpose of the organization is to promote mutual love by bringing together loyal and trustworthy young men and women committed to the principles of seeking the truth and practicing it; to help develop sound character and sacred organization by group training in three areas, the ethical, the physical, and the intellectual; and to build a firm foundation for the future national prosperity.[13]

Dosan Ahn Chang Ho also promoted societal reform by establishing schools, Korean missions, discussion groups, the Friendship Society, and taught the importance of democratic ideals and social change. Dosan built Pachappa Camp based on democratic principals and set up rules and regulations in order to build a harmonious relationship among its Korean residents. Dosan's ultimate goals were to achieve national independence of Korea and to establish the *Gongnip Hyophoe*, the Korean National Association and to join and help lead the Korean Provisional Government in Shanghai. Dosan Ahn Chang Ho ate, slept, and breathed for national independence of his homeland. He was arrested, imprisoned, tortured, and eventually sacrificed himself for the independence of Korea in 1938.

NOTES

1. The original application was submitted to the City's Cultural Heritage Board on February 18, 2015 by UCR History graduate student Hannah Brown, who was also a graduate student researcher at the YOK Center at the time. On May 23, 2016, the application was resubmitted with minor revisions by YOK Center staff and researcher Carol K. Park.

2. The parcels that were designated excluded the parcel 219-321-006, which is owned by the Mobile Oil. Co. The parcel was also part of Pachappa Camp.

3. The team included Erin Gettis, Associate AIA, Principal Planner and City Historic Preservation Officer and Scott Watson, Community & Economic Development, Historic Preservation officer. The outside consultant was Jennifer Mermilliod, M.A., Principal Investigator, Historian/Architectural Historian, JM Research & Consulting.

4. We mainly worked with Lea Petersen, Public Affairs Manager for the Southern California Gas Co. She coordinated the dedication ceremony and worked with her company's leadership to issue press releases and announcements regarding the importance of the designation in terms of Korean American history.

5. "Cultural Point of Interest Recognition for Pachappa Camp P16-0342," Community & Economic Development Department, City of Riverside Presentation. December 6, 2016.

6. Public Comments, City of Riverside Records, File #: 16-3360, Version: 1, Name: CED—P16-0342 Pachappa Camp 12-6-16.

7. Dosan Ahn Chang Ho public Facebook page.

8. November 1, 2016 email between Jennifer Mermilliod, Historian Consultant to the City of Riverside and Philip "Flip" Ahn Cuddy.

9. U.S. Bureau of Census, 1920 California Federal Population Census Schedules—Riverside Co. (Washington DC: Government Printing Office, 1992).

10. Riverside City and County Directory, (Los Angeles: Riverside Directory Company, 1925–1926).

11. Dolores Hayden, *The Power of Place: Urban Landscapes as Public History* (Cambridge, MA, and London: The MIT Press, 1995), 46.

12. Vincent Moses in discussion with the author.

13. Hyung-chan Kim, *Tosan Ahn Ch'ang-Ho: A Profile of Prophetic Patriot.* Tosan Memorial Foundation, 1996: 91–92. Quoted from Ahn Pyeong-wuk, *Tosan sasang* (Tosan's Thought). Seoul: Samyuk ch'ulp'ansa, 1972: 381–383.

Appendix 1

Immigration Superintendent Office, San Francisco, California: 12023, 1924 December 15

Dear Sir—Hereby I enclosed photo of Bolshevist leader your office look out for him. Understand his coming via Honolulu with few day to your harbor.

I want to advised your office this is very important proposition for you. Gentlemen better look out for the B. [olshevist] leader. The person name is C. H. Ahn or Chang Ho Ahn who is due in your city with in few day he is from Shanghai, China via Honolulu. He was over stop Honolulu thence to your city. The person was in this country number of years and he had family in Los Angeles. But he went China for six years and connected with Bolshevist Government all this years he is coming to U.S. now. Widely or Wisely read Bolshevist policies among the oriental in US also Mexico, the headquarter in your city under name Korean National Association also other one is under name Young Korean Academy in Los Angeles. This man leader of both society and he have over five member in San Francisco and other city through the United States and Mexico and Hawaii.

I hoping that you will have special attention with this matter your officer need not make any investigation with Korean National Association or any other person best the way to sending back to China quite as possible without question him. Probably Korean National Association will take the matter because he is leader their society and responsibility. The person which I mention about by KNA. Do not any further investigation the person sending back where he belong so he can spread more Bolshevist policies.

Yours truly,

Kong Wong and Charles Hong Lee

Appendix 2

Sworn statement of AHN CHANG Ho,
Taken before J. B. Brekke, Imigrant Inspector,
K. Bernard Kim, Interpreter,
Veta J Victor, Stenographer,
at the United States Immigration Office, 608 So.
Dearborn Street, Chicago, Illinois, this June 3, 1925.

Q. What is your name?

A. Ahn Chang Ho.

Q. When did you come to the United States last?

A. Landed here December 16, 1924, at San Francisco.

Q. Under what status were you admitted?

A. I was admitted as a Section 6 Traveler. I have a Section 6 certificate is sued
by the commissioner of Foreign Affairs at Shanghai, China

Q. How old are you?

A. 47 Years old.

Q. Where were you born?

A. Puyang-Yang, Korea.

Q. Where did you embark?

A. Shanghai.

Q: Had you resided in Shanghai a long time?

A. About 3 years.

Q. What was you occupation in Shanghai?

A. I was one of the members of the Korean Provisional Government.

Q. Are you still a member of that Provisional Government?

A. No.

Q. What is your present status of occupation?

A. Just traveling.

Q. Where have you traveled since you were admitted at San Francisco?

A. From San Francisco I went to Los Angeles, remained there about two months. From Los Angeles I went to Stockton, Sacramento, Dinuba, Reedley, San Diego, Riverside, Baskerville. On my way from California to Chicago I stopped at Denver then came to Chicago. From Chicago I went to Philadelphia and New York, New Haven, Conn., Boston, Mass., Fall Rivers, Washington, DC, Patterson, NJ, Princeton, then back to New York, then back to Chicago.

Q. What was your object in visiting there different places?

A. For the purpose of a visiting friends and among these friends the majority are students. I visited them on their own request.

Q. Did they request that you just visit them or was it for the purpose of talking to them, making speeches or addresses, or what?

A. I have talked to them both privately and made public addresses among them.

Q. What has been the subject of your addresses?

A. In general I advised them to make a proper preparation for the future freedom and independence of Korea. Among the students I advised them they should work honestly and learn all they can while they had the opportunity and co-operate among the students.

Q. Are you interested in the Soviet Government of Russia?

A. I am not interested directly or indirectly.

Q. Did you talks to the students at their different places in any way involve questions regarding the government of the United States?

A. No.

Q. Are you at all interested in the Government of the United States—that is do you think it is all right as it is, or should it be changed in any way.

A. As far as I can see about the American government I could find no fault.

Q. In the addresses which you have made did you at any time advocate radical changes in the Government of the United States.

A. Never—I know no reason for it.

Q. Is there an association called the Korean national Association?

A. Yes.

Q. For what purpose was that organized/

A. To help the Koreans to help each other.

Q. Is this Korean National Association at any time endeavoring to influence the policy of the Government of the United States?

A. No.

Q. Have you enemies in the United States that you know of?

A. So far as I know I have no enemies. There might be some Koreans who dislike me activities.

Q. What was your real purpose in coming to the United States this last time?

A. It could be covered in three different ways: First, to see my family; Second, to investigate educational work of this country (For the poor students— so they could work part time and go to school part time) I have always been interested in education work. I had been principal of schools in Korea; Third, visiting old friends.

Q. What family have you here?

A. Wife, one brother, two sons and two daughters.

Q. Where are your wife and children at the present time?

A. Los Angeles, 106, Figueroa.

Q. How long do you intend to stay in the United States before returning to Shanghai?

A. Originally I intended to stay for eight months but I would like to stay until next January, providing I get an extension of time granted. (I have permission to remain eight months).

Bibliography

Annual Report of the Board of Home Missions of the Presbyterian Church in the U.S.A. (Presbyterian Church in the U.S.A.: 1918.)

Calvary Presbyterian Church Minutes of Session. Inside the book it says on the cover page: Minutes of the Session of the Presbyterian Church, Presbyterian Board of Publication, No. 1334 Chestnut Street, Philadelphia. Date Range: 6/19/1887–4/2/1906.

Cha, John, Willow Tree Shade: The Susan Ahn Cuddy Story. Korean American Heritage Foundation, 2002.

Chang, Edward T. "What Does It Mean to Be Korean Today?" Part I and II. *Amerasia Journal.* Vol. 29 No. 3, 2003 and Vol. 30. No. 1, 2004.

Chang, Edward T. "*Chosonjok*: Koreans in China" *Amerasia Journal.* Vol. 29 No. 3, 2003.: 37–41.

Chang, Edward T. Translated. *Unsung Hero: The Story of Col. Young Oak Kim.* By Woo Sung Han. Riverside, California: The YOK Center for Korean American Studies, 2011.

Chang, Edward T. and Hannah Brown, "Pachappa Camp: The First Koreatown in the United States," *California History*, 2018: 46–56.

Chang, Edward T. and Jeannette Diaz-Veizades. *Ethnic Peace in the American City: Building Community in Los Angeles and Beyond.* New York: NYU Press, 1999.

Chang, Edward T. and Carol Park. *Korean Americans: A Concise History.* Riverside: Young Oak Kim Center for Korean American Studies, UC Riverside, 2019.

Chang, Edward T. and Woo Sung Han, *Korean American Pioneer Aviators: The Willows Airmen.* Lanham, Lexington Books, 2015.

Cha, John. *Willow Tree Shade: The Susan Ahn Cuddy Story.* Korean American Heritage Foundation, 2002.

Cha, Marn Jai. *Koreans in Central California, 1903–1957: A Study of Settlement and Transnational Politics.* Lanham, MD: University Press of America, 2010.

Charr, Easurk Emsen, *The Golden Mountain: The Autobiography of a Korean Immigrant: 1895–1960.* University of Illinois Press, 1961.

Choy, Bong-Youn. *Koreans in America*. Chicago: Nelson Hall, 1979.

Chung, Angie Y. *Legacies of Struggle: Conflict and Cooperation in Korean American Politics*. Stanford, California: Stanford University Press, 2007.

Chung, Angie Y. *Saving Face: The Emotional Costs of the Asian Immigrant Family Myth*. Rutgers University Press, 2016.

Chung, Angie and Edward T. Chang, "Multiple Oppression Politics: A Strategic Approach to Biracial and Multiracial Coalitions." *Social Justice*. 1998: 80–100.

Daniel, Cletus E., *Bitter Harvest: A History of California Farmworkers, 1870–1941* (Ithaca and London: Cornell University Press).

Gardner, Arthur Leslie, The Korean Nationalist Movement and An Chang-Ho, Advocate of Gradualism. Ph.D. dissertation, University of Hawaii, 1979.

Given, Helen L. *The Korean Community in Los Angeles*. San Francisco: R and E Research Association, 1974.

Hall, Joan H., *A Citrus Legacy. Riverside, California*. Highgrove Press, 1992: 23.

Hayen, Dolores, *The Power of Place: Urban Landscapes as Public History* (Cambridge, MA, and London: The MIT Press, 1995.

Hubler, William Henry. *Koreans in Emlyn: A Community in Transition*. Elkins Park, Pennsylvania: Philip Jaisohn Memorial Papers No. 3, 1977.

Hurh, Won Moo. *The Korean Americans*. Westport, Connecticut: The Greenwood Press, 1998.

Ichioka, Yuji. The Issei: *The World of the First Generation Japanese Immigrants 1885–1924*. New York: The Free Press, 1988.

Ichioka, Yuji. "Japanese Immigrant Response to the 1920 California Alien Land Law." *Agricultural History* 58:2 April 1984: 157–78.

Jo, Moon H. *Korean Immigrants and the Challenge of Adjustment*. Westport, CT: Greenwood Press, 1999.

Jo, Moon H. *Korean Immigrants and the Challenge of Adjustment*. Westport, CT: Greenwood Press, 1999.

Kang, K. Connie. *Home Was the Land of Morning Calm: A Saga of a Korean American Family*. New York: Addison-Wesley, 1995.

Kang, Younghill. *The Grass Roof*. New York: C. Scriber's sons, 1931.

Keller, Nora Okja. *Comfort Women: A Novel*. New York: Viking, 1997.

Kim, Elaine and Eui Young Yu, eds. *East to America: Korean American Life Stories*. New York: New Press, 1996.

Kim, Hyung-chan. Edited. *The Korean Diaspora*. Santa Barbara, California: ABC-Clio, Inc. 1977.

Kim, Hyung-chan. *Tosan Ahn Ch'ang-Ho: A Profile of a Prophetic Patriot*. Seoul: Tosan Memorial Foundation, 1996.

Kim, Illsoo. *New Urban Immigrants: The Korean Community in New York*. Princeton, NJ: Princeton University Press, 1981.

Kim, Katherine Yungmee. *Los Angeles's Koreatown*. Arcadia Publishing, 2011.

Kim, Kwang Chung and Won Moo Hurh, "Korean Americans and the 'Success' Image: A Critique." *Amerasia Journal*. 10 (2) 1983: 3–21.

Kim, Richard S. *Quest for Statehood: Korean Immigrant Nationalism and U.S. Sovereignty 1905–1945*. New York: Oxford University Press, 2011.

Kim, Richard Sukjoo. "Korean Tenant Rice Farming in Glenn County, California 1916–1925: An Economic Niche for an Immigrant Community in Transition. M.A. thesis. UCLA, 1993.

Kim, Ronyoung. *Clay Walls.* Seattle: University of Washington Press, 1986.

Kim, Wayne. The Spirit Led Life: In the Whole Counsel of God. CCAH Press, 2010.

Koh, Hesung Chun. Edited.Korean Diaspora: Central Asia, Northeast Asia and North America. New Haven, Connecticut: East Rock Institute, 2008.

Koreans in America. Korean Christian Scholars Journal No. 2, Spring 1977.

Kwak, Tae-Hwan and Seong Hyong Lee eds. *The Korean-American Community: Present, and Future.* Seul, Korea: Kyungnam University Press, 1990.

Kwon, Ho-Youn editor. *Korean Americans: Conflict and Harmony.* Chicago: North Park College and Theological Seminary, 1994.

Kwon, Ho-Youn and Shin Kim eds. *The Emerging Generation of Korean American*s. Seoul, Korea: Kyung Hee University Press, 1993.

Lee, Helie. *Still Life with Rice.* New York: A Touchstone Book, 1996.

Lee, Ki-baik. *A New History of Korea.* Translated by Edward W. Wagner.A New History of Korea. Cambridge, Mass.: Harvard University Press, 1984.

Lee, Mary Paik. *Quiet Odyssey: A Pioneer Korean Woman in America.* Seattle: University of Washington Press, 1990.

Liem, Channing. *Philip Jaisohn: The First Korean-American—A Forgotten Hero.* Elkins Park, Pennsylvania: The Philip Jaisohn Memorial Foundation, 1984.

Lyu, Kingsley K. "Korean Nationalist Activities in Hawaii and the Continental United States, 1900–1945. Part I: 1900–1919." Amerasia Journal. Vol. 4 No. 1, 1977: 23–90.

Lyu, Kingsley K. "Korean Nationalist Activities in Hawaii and the Continental United States, 1900–1945. Part II: 1919–1945." Amerasia Journal. Vol. 4. No. 2, 1977: 53–100.

Melendy, Brett. *Asians in America: Filipinos, Koreans, and East Indians.* Boston: Twayne Publishers, 1977.

Min, Pyong Gap. *Caught in the Middle: Korean Communities in New York and Los Angeles.* Berkeley and Los Angeles: University of California Press, 1994.

Moon, Hyung June. "The Korean Immigrants in America: The Quest for Identity in the Formative Years 1903–1918." Ph.D. dissertation, University of Nevada, Reno, 1977.

Moon, Tom. Th*is Grim and Savage Game: OSS and the Beginning of U.S. Covert Operations in World War II.* Los Angeles: Burning Gate Press, 1991.

Moses, Vince, "Oranges and Independence: Cornelius Earle Rumsey and Ahn Chang Ho; An Early East-West Alliance in Riverside, 1904–1911," *Riverside Museum Associates News Letter,* June 2000.

Ong, Paul, et. al. *The Widening Divide: Income Inequality and Poverty in Los Angeles.* In Paul Ong, Edna Bonacich and Lucie Cheng eds., The New Asian Immigration in Los Angeles And Global Restructuring. Philadelphia: Temple University Press, 1994.

Pak, Gary. *A Ricepaper Airplane.* Honolulu, Hawaii: University of Hawaii Press, 1998.

Park, Carol. *Memoir of a Cashier: Korean Americans, Racism, and Riots*. Riverside: Young Oak Kim Center for Korean American Studies, 2017.

Park, Jacqueline, "An Ch'angho and the Nationalist Origins of Korean Democracy," (Ph.D. diss., school of Oriental and African Studies, University of London, 1999).

Park, Kyeyoung, *L.A. Rising: Korean Relations with Blacks and Latinos After Civil Unrest*. Lanham: Lexington Books, 2019.

Patterson, Wayne and Hyung Chan Kim, *The Koreans in America, 1882–1974: A Chronology & Fact Book* (Dobbs Ferry, NY, Oceana Publications, 1974).

Patterson, Wayne, *From the Land of Hibiscus: Koreans in Hawai'i, 1903–1950* (Honolulu: University of Hawaii Press, 2007).

Patterson, Wayne. *The Ilse: First-Generation Korean Immigrants in Hawaii, 1903–1973*. Honolulu: University of Hawaii Press, 2000.

Patterson, Wayne. *The Korean Frontier in America: Immigration to Hawaii, 1896–1910*. Honolulu: University of Hawaii Press, 1988.

Shin, Linda. "Koreans In America, 1903–1945." *Amerasia Journal*. Vol. 1 No. 3, 1971: 32–39.

Skoggard, Ian. "Talking Diaspora." In *Japanese Studies Around the World 2005*. Kyoto, Japan: International Research Center for Japanese Studies, 2006: 35–52.

Stetz, Margaret and Bonnie B. C. Oh eds. *Legacies of the Comfort Women of World War II*. New York, An East Gate Book, 2001.

Stewart, Patricia, *Fairmont Park: Riverside's Treasure*. Riverside, Ca: 2005.

Sunoo, Harold Hakwon and Sonia Shin Sunoo. "The Heritage of the First Korean Women Immigrants in the United States: 1903–1924." In *Koreans in America*. Korean Christian Scholars Journal No. 2, Spring 1977: 142–171.

Sunoo, Sonia. "Korean Women Pioneers of the Pacific Northwest." *Oregon Historical Quarterly*. 79: 51–64.

Sunoo, Sonia Shinn. *Korea Kaleidoscope: Oral Histories, Volume One Early Korean Pioneers in USA*: 1903–1905. Sierra Mission Area: United States Presbyterian Church, 1982.

Takaki, Ronald. *Strangers From a Different Shore*. Boston: Little, Brown and Company, 1989.

Thun, Ellen, *Heartwarmers*: Afterward: Change, February 25, 1997.

Thun, Ellen, "Heartwarmers: Annexation," *Korea Times*. January 28, 1997.

Wales, Nym and Kim San, *Song of Ariran: A Korean Communist in the Chinese Revolution*. San Francisco: Ramparts Press, Inc., 1941: 120. Quoted from Hyun-Chan Kim, 1996.

Wampler, Molly Frick. *Not Without Honor: The Story of Sammy Lee*. Santa Barbara, California: Fithian Press, 1987.

Yoo, David K. *Contentious Spirits: Religion in Korean American History, 1903–1945*. Stanford: Stanford University Press, 2010.

Yoo, Jay Kun. *The Koreans in Seattle*. Elkins Park, Pennsylvania: Philip Jaisohn Memorial Papers No. 4. 1979.

Yoon, In-Jin. *On My Own: Korean Businesses and Race Relations in America*. Chicago: University of Chicago Press, 1997.

Yoon, In-Jin. *The Social Origin of Korean Immigration to the United States from 1965 to the Present*. Honolulu: East-West Population Institute, 1993.

Yoon, Won Kil. *Global Pulls on The Korean Communities in Sao Paulo and Buenos Aires*. Lanham: Lexington Books, 2015.

Yoon, Won Kil. *The Passage of a Picture Bride*. Loma Linda: Loma Linda University Press, 1989.

Yu, Eui-Young and Edward T. Chang eds. *Multiethnic Coalition Building in Los Angeles*. Los Angeles: Koryo Research Institute, 1995.

Yu, Eui-Young. "Korean Communities in America: Past, Present, and Future." *Amerasia Journal*. Vol. 10 No. 2: 23–51.

Yu, Eui-Young. *Korean Community Profile: Life and Consumer Patterns*. Los Angeles: Korea Times, 1990.

Yun, Yo-jun. "Early History of Korean Immigration to America," in *The Korean Diaspora*, ed. by Hyung-Chan Kim. Santa Barbara: CLIO Press, 1979.

KOREAN LANGUAGE SOURCES

Ahn, Hyung Joo. "Syngman Rhee and Education of Young Hawaii Korean (1913–1923). In Miju Hanin Wei Minjok Woondong (Korean Americans and Their Struggles for National Independence). Seoul, Korea: Yonsei University, 2003.

Ahn, Jin. Mi Kunjung Kwa Hankuk wei Minju Juwei: American Military Government in Korea and Democracy. Paju, Korea: Hanul Academy, 2005.

Ban, Byung Ryul. Miju Ji Yok E-Seo-Wei Muryuk Yangsung Woondong (Armed Resistance Movement in North America). In Miju Hanin Wei Minjok Woondong (Korean Americans and Their Struggles for National Independence). Seoul, Korea: Yonsei University, 2003.

Chang, Tae Han translated. *Lonesome Journey*. By K. W. Lee, Luke and Grace Kim eds. Seoul, Korea: Korea University Press, 2016.

Chu, Yo-han, Ahn Tosan Cheonseo (The Complete Works of Ahn Ch'ang-ho), (Seoul: Samchungtang, 1963), 48.

Dosan-Hak Yeon-Gu: Dosan-Hak Yeon-Gu: A Study of Dosan. Dosan Studies Association. Vol. 10, 2004.

Han, See Joon. Han'guk Kwangbokkun yŏn'gu: A Study on Korean Kwang-bok Army. Seoul: Ilchogak, 1993.

Hong, Sun Pyo. Jaemi Hanin-wei Ggum-gwa Dojeon. (Korean American Dreams and Challenges). Seoul: Yonsei University Press, 2011.

Kim, Do Hyung, "Dosan Ahn Chang Ho's Independence Activities through his Passport" 37th The Dosan Society conference,

Kim, Sukjun. MiKunjung Si Dae Wei Kukga Wa Hangjung: Nation and Administration during American Military Government Period. Seoul: Ewha Women's University Press, 1996.

Kim, Won Young. JaeMi Hanin O-Sip Nyn Sa: Fifty-year History of Korean Immigration to the U.S. Seoul: Hyean, 2004.

Koh, Jung Hew. "Chogi Hanin Sahoe-Wa Minjok Woondong (The Early Korean Immigrant Community and Nationalist Movement)" in Pukmiju Hanin Eu Ryoksa: Korean Experience in North America.Vol. 1. Seoul: National Institute of Korean History, 2007: 45–74.

Kwak, Rim Dae. Ahn Dosan. Korean Studies. Vol. 4, 1992.

Lee, Dukhee. Hawaii Hanin Duli Hawaii Gamri Gyohoe-e Ggichin Younghyang: 1903–1952 (How Koreans in Hawaii influenced Methodist Church in Hawaii). Seoul: Korea, National Institute of Korean History, 2003.

Lee, Ja Kyung. Jung-Ga-Ju Chogi Hanin I-Min-Sa GaeYo (Overview of Korean Immigration to Central California). In Miju Jiyok Hanin I-min-sa. Seoul: Korea. National Institute of Korean History, 2003: 127–157.

Lee, Kwang Soo, *Dosan Ahn Chang Ho* (Seoul: HeungSaDan, 1947).

Lee, Sun Joo. "The Role of DosanAhn Chang Ho in Riverside: 1904–1914." In The Movement and Its Outgrowth by Korean Americans." Los Angeles: Centennial Committee of Korean Immigration to the U.S. 2003, 111–192.

Lee, Kwang Kyu. JaeMi Hankookin (Korean American). Seoul, Korea: Iljokak, 1989.

Lee, Kwang Soo. Dosan Ahn Chang Ho. Seoul: Heung Sa Dan, 1978.

Lee, Man-yeol. "Miju Hanin Gyohoe-Wa Dokrip Woondong (Korean American Church and Independence Movement)" in Miju Hanin Wei Minjok Woondong (Korean Americans and Their Struggles for National Independence). Seoul, Korea: Yonsei University, 2003: 63–111.

Lee, Sunju, "Dosan Ahn Chang Ho's Activities in Riverside: 1904–1914," in *The Independence Movement and its Outgrowth by Korean Americans* (Los Angeles: Centennial Committee of Korean Immigration to the U.S., 2003).

Miju Hanin Chil-Sip-Nyn-Sa: Seventy Year History of Korean American Community. Seoul: Overseas Korean Studies Center, 1973.

Miju Hanin Wei Minjok Woondong (Korean Americans and Their Struggles for National Independence). Seoul, Korea: Yonsei University, 2003.

Miju Jiyok Hanin I-min-sa. Seoul: Korea. National Institute of Korean History, 2003.

Oh, In Whan and Jung Ja Kong. Gu Han-mal Hanin Hawaii I-Min (Korean Migration to Hawaii) Incheon, Korea: Inha University Press, 2004.

Pang, Sun Joo. Jaemi Hanin Wei Dokrip Woondong (Independence Movement in the United States). Chunchon, Korea: Han-lim University Press, 1989.

Pang, Sun Joo. "Hanin Mikook I-ju-eu Si-jak" (The Beginning of the Korean Migration to the United States). In Miju Jiyok Hanin I-min-sa. Seoul: Korea. National Institute of Korean History, 2003: 53–75.

Park, Hwan. 20 Segi Hankook KeunHyun DaeSa Yeongu-wa Jangjum (Korean Modern History Seoul: Kukhak Jaryo Won, 2001.

Pukmiju Hanin Eu Ryoksa: Korean Experience in North America.Vol. I and II. Seoul: National Institute of Korean History, 2007.

Yoon, In-jin. Korean Diaspora. Seoul, Korea: Korea University Press, 2004.

ARCHIVES, COLLECTIONS, AND PRIVATE PAPERS

Calvary Presbyterian Church 125th Anniversary Celebration Worship Heritage Sunday June 24, 2012.

Interview with Ellen Thun by Edward T. Chang in Riverside on July 1, 1992.

Interview with Ellen Thun by Edward T. Chang on February 23, 1993, at her apartment in Los Angeles.

Naeri Church Record, Incheon, Korea [D01.97] National Archive and Record Administration (NARA).

Riverside City and County Directory, (Los Angeles: Riverside Directory Company, 1925–1926).

U.S. Census Bureau Record, January 20, 1920.

U.S. Department of Labor District No. 30, Immigration Service, Office of the Commissioner Angel Island Station Via Ferry Post Office, December 24, 1924.

U.S. Department of Labor, Immigration Service, Office of the Commissioner Angel Island Station Via Ferry Post Office, December 24, 1924. Document No. 238880/1-6. Investigation Arrival Case Files, San Francisco, Records of the U.S. Immigration and Naturalization Service, RG 85, National Archives, Pacific Region, San Bruno, Ca.

U.S. Department of Labor, Immigration Service, Office of Inspector in Chicago, Ill. April 28, 1925. Document No. 2008/967.

U.S. Department of Labor, Immigration Service, Office of District Director Los Angeles, Calif. May 11, 1925. Document No. 25140/24.

U.S. Department of Labor, Immigration Service, Office of the Commissioner Angel Island Station Via Ferry Post Office, June 26, 1925. Document No. 12025/02.

U.S. Department of Labor, Bureau of Immigration, Washington. July 11, 1925. Document No. 55466/466.

U.S. Department of Labor, Immigration Service, Office of the Commissioner Angel Island Station Via Ferry Post Office February 23, 1926. Document No. 12025/14120.

U.S. Bureau of Census, 1920 California Federal Population Census Schedules—Riverside Co. (Washington DC: Government Printing Office, 1992).

NEWSPAPERS AND PERIODICALS

Gong Rip Sinbo

Hemet News, June 27, 1913: "train from Riverside brought about twenty Korean laborers."

Hemet News, July 4, 1913: "11 Korean fruit pickers."

Hemet News, July 11, 1913: "Korean laborers comes from Los Angeles."

Korea Daily, Los Angeles.

Los Angeles Herald, March 24, 1908.

Los Angeles Times, June 27, 1913: "The noon train from Los Angeles brought twenty-five or thirty Japanese and Koreans, who had been employed by one of the Koreans to handle the apricot crop of the local rancher."

Los Angeles Times, June 28, 1913: "a party of Korean apricot pickers from Riverside."

Los Angeles Times, July 2, 1913, p. 14; *Hemet News,* July 4, 1913, p. 1; "Hemet Incident Considered Closed."

New Korea (*Sinhan Minbo*)

Press Enterprise, March 6, 1921: 6.

Riverside Daily Press, March 22, 1905: 8.

Riverside (Enterprise), June 26, 1913: "About twenty Japanese and Koreans" from Riverside.

Riverside Enterprise, June 30, 1913: "The spokesman then said, 'All right get our tickets and we will return to Los Angeles.'"

Riverside Enterprise, June 30, 1913: "They were not wanted and should return to Los Angeles."

Riverside Daily Press, July 2, 1913, p. 2.

Riverside Daily Press, October 20, 1905: 8.

San Francisco Chronicle, "Corea: The Sleeping Land" December 7, 1902.

San Jacinto Register, June 26, 1913: "15 Japs."

San Francisco Call, June 27, 1913: "15 Korean fruit pickers," "apricot picking crew of Koreans from Riverside"; *San Francisco Call,* 28 June 1913: "Korean apricot pickers from Riverside."

The Independent.

Index

About the Author

Edward T. Chang is professor of ethnic studies and founding director of the Young Oak Kim Center for Korean American Studies at the University of California at Riverside. A prolific researcher, Professor Chang has published eleven books, seven edited volumes, and numerous articles. In 2019, he published "Korean Americans: A Concise History" and "Pachappa Camp: The First Koreatown in the United States" in 2018. Also, in 2015, Lexington Books published: *Korean American Pioneer Aviators: The Willows Airmen*. Professor Chang has studied and been a voice of the Korean community for more than twenty-five years. He is a leading expert on the Los Angeles civil unrest, race relations between Korean and African American communities, and Korean Americans. Professor Chang lectures on the topics of Korean-African American Relations and the Los Angeles civil unrest and its impact on the Korean American community nationally and internationally. Chang received the "Order of Civil Merit, Magnolia Medal" from the Republic of Korea in 2019, and the "Grand Prize" from the Association for the Studies of Koreans Abroad in 2019. Chang is a board member of the Council of Korean Americans and Adviser of the Overseas Koreans Foundation.